D1570684

PRAGMATICS IN SPEECH AND LANGUAGE PATHOLOGY

STUDIES IN SPEECH PATHOLOGY
AND CLINICAL LINGUISTICS

AIMS AND SCOPE

The establishment of this series reflects the growth of both interest and research into disorders of speech and language. It is intended that the series will provide a platform for the development of academic debate and enquiry into the related fields of speech pathology and clinical linguistics.
To this end, the series will publish book length studies or collections of papers on aspects of disordered communication, and the relation between language theory and language pathology.

Volume 7

Nicole Müller (ed.)

Pragmatics in Speech and Language Pathology
Studies in clinical applications

PRAGMATICS IN SPEECH AND LANGUAGE PATHOLOGY

STUDIES IN CLINICAL APPLICATIONS

Edited by

NICOLE MÜLLER
Cardiff University

JOHN BENJAMINS PUBLISHING COMPANY
AMSTERDAM/PHILADELPHIA

TM

The paper used in this publication meets the minimum requirements of American National Standard for Information Sciences — Permanence of Paper for Printed Library Materials, ANSI Z39.48-1984.

Library of Congress Cataloging-in-Publication Data

Pragmatics in speech and language pathology / edited by Nicole Müller.
    p.   cm. -- (Studies in speech pathology and clinical linguistics, ISSN 0927-1813, v. 7)
    Includes bibliographical references and index.
    1. Speech disorders. 2. Pragmatics. 3. Speech therapy. I. Müller, Nicole, 1962- II. Series.
RC423.A2 P76   2000
616.85'5--dc21   00-021033
ISBN 90 272 4338 7 (Eur.) / 1 55619 274 6 (US) (Hb; alk. paper)

John Benjamins Publishing Co. • P.O.Box 75577 • 1070 AN Amsterdam • The Netherlands
John Benjamins North America • P.O.Box 27519 • Philadelphia PA 19118-0519 • USA

Table of Contents

List of Contributors

Martin J. Ball
School of Psychology and
Communication, University of
Ulster, Northern Ireland

Stephen N. Camarata
Department of Hearing and Speech
Sciences, Vanderbilt University
Medical Center, Nashville, USA

Alison Ferguson
Department of Linguistics,
University of Newcastle, Newcastle,
NSW, Australia

Lorraine McAnulty
Down and Lisburn Health and
Social Services Trust,
Northern Ireland

Kay Mogford-Bevan
Bodmin Hill, Lostwithiel, Cornwall,
UK

Nicole Müller
Centre for Language and
Communication Research, Cardiff
University, Cardiff, Wales, UK

Claire Penn
Department of Speech Pathology
and Audiology, University of the
Witwatersrand, Johannesburg, South
Africa

Michael R. Perkins
Department of Human
Communication Science, University
of Sheffield, Sheffield, UK

Amanda Willcox
North Durham Community Health
Care Trust, Durham, UK

John Wilson
School of Psychology and
Communication, University of
Ulster, Northern Ireland

Pragmatics in Speech and Language Pathology
Clinical Pragmatics

Nicole Müller
Cardiff University

Since its establishment as a distinct discipline of study, the field of clinical linguistics and phonetics has faced a dual challenge: on the one hand, to use the methods of linguistics and phonetics to investigate disordered speech and language and thus to inform clinical assessment and intervention, and on the other hand, to inform theory formation and the extension of the available knowledge base in general linguistics and phonetics through the analysis of disordered speech and language. The twofold challenge confronted by pragmatics in speech and language pathology, or clinical pragmatics (whether one regards it as a subdiscipline of clinical linguistics, or an extension thereof, or as an independent discipline in its own right), may be formulated in a similar way: to use the methods of pragmatics to investigate disordered (linguistic) human interaction (and thus to contribute to the development of clinical practice) on the one hand, and on the other, to contribute to the elucidation of human linguistic interaction in general through the analysis of disordered data.

At this stage, one may well ask what the methods of pragmatics, mentioned above, are. As every student of pragmatics is aware, the definitions of the term, and consequently of the field of study, are many and varied. In particular newcomers to the field may be excused if the apparent lack of one cogent, snappy definition fills them with unease, especially when faced with subdisciplines such as cognitive pragmatics (see Kasher 1998a), or modular pragmatics (see Kasher 1998b), clinical pragmatics, pragmatic disability, or indeed semantic-pragmatic disorder. In addition, the dual reality of pragmatics in the field, as it were, i.e. in the context of speech and language pathology practice, may very well add to theoretical and terminological confusion, since we are dealing both with an applied science, and with the science of application.

The study of pragmatics in a speech and language pathology context experienced a considerable rise in interest in the 1980s and 1990s (see e.g. Gallagher and Prutting 1983, Grunwell and James 1989 for earlier contributions to the area). This interest has, at this time, by no means abated (witness recent collection such as Paradis 1998), despite, or maybe even because of, an often perceived lack of coherence and concentration in both methodology and data analysed (see also e.g. Perkins's and Penn's contributions to this volume).

This book does not attempt to provide yet another (working) definition of the field of pragmatics, nor is it intended as a textbook of clinical pragmatics. There are many good pragmatics textbooks available (e.g. Grundy 1995, Levinson 1983, Mey 1993, to name only a few), as well as introductory volumes aimed more specifically at the speech and language pathology community (e.g. McTear and Conti-Ramsden 1991, Smith and Leinonen 1992). Our aim is to bring together theoretical aspects of the study of pragmatics in a clinical context, as well as practical applications of theory in clinical assessment and intervention.

The contributions in this book meet the dual challenge outlined above in very different ways. Perkins (Chapter 2) addresses the problematicity of applying methods and concepts developed in linguistic pragmatics to disordered communication, which has led to an "overly narrow linguistic bias" in the study of pragmatic disability (p. 8). Perkins approaches pragmatic disability in terms of "an imbalance between a range of underlying cognitive systems" (ibid.), from a perspective more grounded in cognitive science than linguistic pragmatics, and contributes his own definition of pragmatic ability, namely that it is "most usefully seen as an epiphenomenal consequence of the way in which linguistic and nonlinguistic cognitive systems interact" (p. 10). He proposes a classification system of "primary pragmatic disability" (due to non-linguistic cognitive dysfunction) and "secondary pragmatic disability" (due to linguistic or sensorimotor dysfunction).

Chapter 3 presents a further reflection on and application of research in cognitive science. Wilson and McAnulty express their unease with the term semantic-pragmatic disorder (see e.g. Rapin and Allen 1983, 1998) as a diagnostic label for forms of conversational disability in children. They locate pragmatic impairment (their preferred term) as "residing at the cognitive/communication interface (p. 33), and draw upon Baron-Cohen's theory of mind model (see e.g. Baron-Cohen 1995), and also on work in artificial intelligence, i.e. Ballim and Wilks's model of artificial believers, in a contribution which focuses on problems with referential and topic construction.

Ferguson (Chapter 4) reviews notions of communication strategies and proposes a model of strategic communication. Central to the discussion is the contrasting of perspectives on language in psycholinguistics and sociolinguistics, and the concept and role of context in communication. The view of language taken in this chapter is as "the joint product of individuals continuously influenced by their socio-cultural environment" (p. 58); meanings are not static, but are negotiated by partners in a multilayered and dynamic process. Although the chapter uses examples from aphasia and aphasia-therapy as illustrations, the notions explored should be applicable to many different areas of disordered communication, and should be of particular interest to readers who are interested in comparing and contrasting the merits of different theoretical approaches to language and language use as applied to disordered communication, such as Systemic Functional Linguistics (e.g. Halliday 1985) and Conversation Analysis (e.g. Atkinson and Heritage 1984; Sacks, Schegloff and Jefferson 1974).

Ball's contribution (Chapter 5) centres on issues of pragmatic profiling in aphasia, and difficulties associated with profile-type approaches to pragmatic ability, focusing particulary on the Pragmatic Protocol (Prutting and Kirchner 1983, 1987) and the Profile of Communicative Appropriateness (Penn 1988). The analysis concentrates on inter-scorer consistency, and the difference between two-point and five-point scales. Some of the difficulties arising in profiling pragmatics (e.g. discrepancies in inter-scorer reliability) can be seen to be grounded in the application of an assessment type which was originally developed for areas of language assessment where judgments of acceptability are generally much more straightforward than in pragmatics (i.e. syntax/morphology and phonology). In order to overcome these difficulties, and to make full use of available protocols, appropriate training of clinicians is of the utmost importance.

Penn (Chapter 6) presents a stocktaking of some twenty years of clinical pragmatics, pragmatic approaches in the field of clinical language analysis, and pragmatic assessment tools, again with particular focus on aphasia. Penn develops a model of Explanation and Relevance which integrates the notions of impairment, disability and handicap with pragmatic assessment and various types of pragmatic measurement tools, with the issues of explanation and relevance, which in turn should guide both assessment and therapy. Penn also addresses issues of a functional skills focus and outcome measurement in therapy and their need to be reconciled with a pragmatic approach.

Willcox and Mogford-Bevan (Chapter 7) present a paediatric case study of pragmatic difficulty. The conversations of a child in the environment of a language unit are analysed, and it emerges that the child shows atypical behaviours in the areas of attention getting devices, initiations, directives, responses, cohesion, and repair. The report on intervention focuses on progress in the child's handling of initiations.

The focus of Camarata's contribution (Chapter 8) is different from any of the other chapters in this book, in as much as it investigates the pragmatics of language intervention, rather than assessment or treatment of pragmatic disorders. The author reviews six paediatric language intervention programmes widely used with preschool to early school age children. Each programme is presented according to a common pattern: a description of the intervention is followed by an example of clinical interaction, an evaluation of the pragmatic aspects of the intervention, and a comparison of the pragmatics of the intervention to the pragmatics of more general, natural (as opposed to clinical) contexts. Thus Camarata points up yet another facet in the wide remit of clinical pragmatics, i.e. the pragmatics of the speech and language clinic.

References

Atkinson, J. M. and Heritage, J. (eds) 1984. *Sructures of Social Action: Studies in Conversation Analysis*. Cambridge University Press.
Ballim, A. and Wilks, Y. 1992. *Artificial Believers*. Hove: LEA.
Baron-Cohen, S. 1995. *Mindblindness: An Essay on Autism and Theory and Mind*. Cambridge, Mass: MIT Press.
Gallagher, T. and Prutting, C. 1983. *Issues in Pragmatic Assessment and Intervention in Language*. San Diego: College Hill.
Grundy, P. 1995. *Doing Pragmatics*. London: Edward Arnold.
Grunwell, P. and James, A. 1989. *The Functional Evaluation of Language Disability*. London: Croom Helm.
Halliday, M. A. K. 1985. *An Introduction to Functional Grammar*. London: Edward Arnold.
Kasher, A. 1998a. "Pragmatics, cognitive". In *Concise Encyclopedia of Pragmatics*, J. Mey (ed.), 737–739.
———— 1998b. "Pragmatics, modular". In *Concise Encyclopedia of Pragmatics*, J. Mey (ed.), 738–739.
Levinson, S. C. 1983. *Pragmatics*. Cambridge: Cambridge University Press.
McTear, M. and Conti-Ramsden, G. 1991. *Pragmatic Disability in Children: Assessment and Intervention*. London: Whurr.
Mey, J. L. 1993. *Pragmatics: An Introduction*. Oxford: Blackwell.
Paradis, M. (ed.) 1998. *Pragmatics in Neurogenic Communication Disorders*. Oxford: Pergamon.
Penn, C. 1988. "The profiling of syntax and pragmatics in aphasia". *Clinical Linguistics and Phonetics* 2: 179–207.

Prutting, C. and Kirchner, D. 1983. "Applied pragmatics". In *Pragmatic Assessment and Intervention Issues in Language*, T. Gallagher and C. Prutting (eds). San Diego: College Hill.

Prutting, C. and Kirchner, D. 1987. "A clinical appraisal of the pragmatic aspects of language". *Journal of Speech and Hearing Disorders* 52, 105–19.

Rapin, I. and Allen, D. A. 1983. "Developmental Language Disorders: Nosologic considerations". In *Neuropsychology of Language, Reading and Spelling*, U. Kirk (ed.), 155–184. New York: Academic Press.

——— 1998. "The semantic-pragmatic deficit disorder: classification issues". *International Journal of Language and Communication Disorders* 33 (1): 82–87.

Sacks, H., Schegloff, E. and Jefferson, G. 1974. "A simplest systematics for the organization of turn taking for conversation". *Language* 50: 696–735.

Smith, B. R. and Leinonen, E. 1992. *Clinical Pragmatics*. London: Chapman and Hall.

The Scope of Pragmatic Disability
A Cognitive Approach

Michael R. Perkins

University of Sheffield

1. Introduction

Clinicians have long been aware of the distinction between specific speech and language impairments on the one hand, and communicative ability on the other. We all know of aphasic individuals who are successful communicators in spite of their linguistic difficulties, as well as other individuals, perhaps with right brain damage or high level autism, who are poor communicators in spite of all the appearances of having a relatively intact linguistic system. It is only in more recent years, however, that terms such as pragmatic ability and pragmatic disability have come to be used to describe cases such as these latter ones (see, for example, Gallagher 1991; McTear and Conti-Ramsden 1992; Smith and Leinonen 1992). What advantages has this brought us? The obvious gains are that we now have at our disposal the fruits of many years of research in linguistics and the philosophy of language, in the form of a set of theoretical and descriptive categories which enable us to be far more discerning in the types of communicative behaviour we can identify. Terms such as speech act, illocutionary force, implicature, maxims of conversation, presupposition, deixis and relevance are commonplace in the language pathology literature. Such gains have been bought at a price, however. Along with the terminology has come a great deal of theoretical baggage which was not developed with communication impairment in mind, and one would hardly have expected its direct application to the clinical domain to be entirely unproblematic. It is perhaps surprising, therefore, to find that this issue has rarely been addressed, and that the wholesale importation of pragmatic theories into the clinical domain has largely gone unquestioned.

In this chapter I will argue that the direct and unmodified application of frameworks and concepts from linguistic pragmatics to the study of communicative impairment has introduced an overly narrow linguistic bias which, despite the undoubted insights it provides, has so far been of limited clinical value. I will outline instead an alternative approach to describing and understanding pragmatic disability which has more in common with cognitive science than pragmatic theory, and which accounts for impaired communicative behaviour in terms of an imbalance between a range of underlying cognitive systems. As well as making it possible to distinguish between different types of pragmatic disability in cognitive terms, this approach has the potential to clarify and facilitate the remedial task of the clinician by targetting the causes of pragmatic impairment instead of merely focusing on its behavioural symptoms.

2.   Approaches to Clinical Pragmatics

One problem with identifying a programme for clinical pragmatics is that the discipline of pragmatics itself lacks coherence. Indeed, Horn (1988: 113) describes it as "a large, loose, and disorganized collection of research efforts", and descriptions of pragmatic disability turn out to be similarly diverse and inconsistent. For example, there is considerable overlap between the terms 'pragmatics' and 'discourse'[1] and similar types of disability may be described almost arbitrarily under either heading. Much work on acquired disorders in adults uses the term 'discourse disability' (e.g. Chapman and Ulatowska 1989; Joanette and Brownell 1990; Bloom, Obler, De Santi and Ehrlich 1994) whereas the developmental literature appears on the whole[2] to prefer the term 'pragmatic disability' (e.g. Roth and Spekman 1984; McTear and Conti-Ramsden 1992; Craig 1995). Some researchers have opted for a particular theoretical framework such as speech act theory (Lucas 1980; Hirst, LeDoux and Stein 1984; Loveland, Landry, Hughes, Hall and McEvoy 1988; McDonald 1992), Gricean implicature (Damico 1985; Ahlsén 1993), conversation analysis (Local and Wootton 1995; Willcox and Mogford-Bevan 1995; Ferguson 1996), relevance theory (Frith 1989; Happé 1991; Happé 1993) or cohesion analysis (Wykes and Leff 1982; Ripich and Terrell 1988; Armstrong 1991), though in many cases the phenomena described could have been accounted for equally well using alternative frameworks. Others have attempted to encompass such terminological and theoretical heterogeneity by devising comprehensive checklists or profiles for describing pragmatic disability. Prutting and Kirchner's (1983) Pragmatic Protocol includes seven general categories (speech acts, topic, turn taking, lexical selection, stylistic variation, intelligibility and prosodics, kinesics and proxemics) which are broken down into a further thirty subcategories. Penn (1985) in her Profile of Communicative Appropriateness slices the cake somewhat differently. Her six superordinate categories are: response to interlocutor, control of semantic content, cohesion, fluency, sociolinguistic sensitivity and non-verbal communication, and these are divided into a further fifty one subcategories. Although both checklists have been used successfully to characterise and distinguish different impaired populations (e.g. Prutting and Kirchner 1987; Penn 1988), it is evident from comparing them that their criteria for what counts as pragmatic disability are somewhat arbitrary, and certainly do not include theoretical consistency or coherence (see the chapter by Martin Ball in this volume).

3.   A Cognitive Approach to Pragmatics

A major problem for pragmatics as a discipline lies in its breadth and heterogeneity. Without wishing to go over yet again the old ground of how pragmatics should be defined (see Levinson 1983 for a good discussion), at its broadest pragmatics can be seen as having to do with how language is used in the process of communication. Pragmatic theorists have for the most part considered language use in linguistic, sociological or philosophical terms — e.g. what are the characteristics of language in use, and what are the sociolinguistic and logical principles which govern it? An alternative way of approaching pragmatics, and the one I will be proposing here as being particularly apposite for clinical applications, is to consider what determines language use in psychological terms. More specifically, what are the various cognitive systems and processes which underlie and contribute to language behaviour. Such an approach (under the name of cognitive neuropsychology) has proved extremely useful in aphasiology and has enabled therapy programmes to be far more specifically focused with clear benefits for remedial outcome (see, for example, Morris and Franklin 1995). So far, however, there have been very few attempts to look at pragmatic ability and disability from a cognitive perspective. Some have assumed rather simplistically that pragmatics constitutes a single separate cognitive 'module',[3] on a par with — though distinct from — syntax, morphology, phonology and semantics (see, for example, the discussion in Craig 1995). Kasher (1991; 1994), on the other hand, argues that pragmatics covers too wide a range of phenomena to be a single cognitive system. He does, however, suggest that certain pragmatic phenomena such as specific types of speech act are modular, but that others such as conversational implicature are not, in that they are instances of more general principles which are not restricted to language alone. It is interesting to note, though, that the various pragmatic phenomena Kasher entertains as possible candidates for pragmatic modules are invariably defined using the terminology of standard pragmatic theory which is not cognitively biased. Wilson and Sperber (1991), whose Relevance Theory *is* a serious attempt to ground pragmatics in cognition, come closest to the view to be adopted here. They argue that pragmatics is not a primary cognitive module at all, but rather "the domain in which grammar, logic and memory interact" (p. 583). My own view is that pragmatic ability is most usefully seen as an epiphenomenal consequence of the way in which linguistic and nonlinguistic cognitive systems interact. In other words, phenomena such as speech acts, conversational maxims, and so on, are not primary cognitive entities themselves but are instead the secondary consequences of interactions between more fundamental cognitive systems (Perkins 1998). The reason why we have come to regard such abstract constructs as primary entities, worthy of consideration as cognitive modules, is simply that they have been deemed such by pragmatic theorists who have not generally been particularly interested in, and therefore constrained by, the way human cognition operates.

Figure 1 is a schematic summary of the cognitive and sensorimotor bases of pragmatics. The linguistic cognitive systems shown provide us with the means of encoding and decoding meaning. The nonlinguistic cognitive systems interact with the linguistic systems to determine the what, why, when, where and how of the encoding and decoding processes. The sensorimotor input and output systems allow for the transmission and reception of linguistic information via different modalities.

PRAGMATIC ABILITY

Linguistic systems	Nonlinguistic systems	
Cognitive systems		*Sensory and motor input & output systems*
prosody phonology morphology syntax lexis	inferential ability social cognition theory of mind executive function memory affect world knowledge	vocal-auditory visual tactile

Figure 1. *Schematic summary of the cognitive and sensorimotor bases of pragmatics*

So how does interaction between these various systems determine what we understand by pragmatics? Let me give an example. Mary and John are conversing. They have a range of choices available for encoding what they want to say at each linguistic level. For example their vocabulary can be formal or informal; pedantic or poetic. Their syntax can be simple or complex. They may 'upgrade' their phonological system to RP or 'downgrade' it to educated Brummie. They may vary their intonation, tempo and loudness. In addition, there is the potential for complex interplay between linguistic levels. For example, they may choose to request assent or dissent explicitly via syntax (Would you like some tea?) or prosody (Téa?) or purely implicitly (There's some tea in the pot). Although the range of choices available is generated by the linguistic system itself, the specific choices made on any given occasion are determined at least partly by non-linguistic considerations. For example: what Mary knows about John and how much she remembers of it; what she is able to infer about his beliefs and emotions; what beliefs and emotions of her own she intends to convey; how closely she is able to monitor her own and John's communicative behaviour including their mutual awareness; what particular rules of social engagement she wishes to play by and how closely she intends to stick to them. In addition, there is also choice regarding the distribution of information across different modalities — i.e. the vocal-auditory, visual or even tactile channels. In short, the formal properties of any utterance are jointly determined by the generative capacity of the linguistic system and the varying states of a range of nonlinguistic cognitive and sensorimotor systems. The actual communicative behaviours themselves can be characterised in various ways according to one's preferred linguistic and pragmatic theory. For example, the decision not to linguistically encode 'request for assent/dissent' in the sentence 'There's some tea in the pot' can be seen as being consistent with a politeness principle, or described in terms of an indirect speech act, a flouting of the maxim of manner, and so on. To do so, however, obscures the underlying cognitive aetiology of such behaviour.

The shift of emphasis from communicative behaviour to underlying cognitive capacity is particularly useful in the characterisation of pragmatic disability. It is important to be able to specify whether such disability is a result of (a) a nonlinguistic impairment, (b) a linguistic impairment or (c) some combination of both. Separate instances of communicative impairment may appear superficially similar and yet have distinct underlying causes. For example, one problem with the use of a diagnostic label such as 'semantic-pragmatic disorder' (Rapin and Allen 1983) is that sometimes one finds it used to describe poor conversational performance resulting from sociocognitive dysfunction (i.e. nonlinguistic impairment), and at others to describe similar behaviour caused by problems with lexical access and sentence formulation (i.e. linguistic impairment).[4]

In the remainder of this chapter I will propose a classification scheme for pragmatic disability, based on the approach outlined above, which is intended to clarify what we mean by pragmatic disability and to reduce some of the confusion which currently exists in this area. I will distinguish between disorders of language use which are due to nonlinguistic cognitive dysfunction (primary pragmatic disability), and those which are due to linguistic or sensorimotor dysfunction (secondary pragmatic disability). Finally I will discuss disorders which are due to both linguistic and nonlinguistic dysfunction (complex pragmatic disability). Most space will be devoted to primary pragmatic disability since this represents the most novel aspect of the framework and also accounts for those impairments which have been most commonly labelled as instances of pragmatic disability.

4.   Primary Pragmatic Disability

I will use the term *Primary Pragmatic Disability* (PPD) to refer to a condition in which the linguistic system (i.e. phonology, prosody, morphology, syntax, lexis) is essentially intact, but where communicative performance is impaired as a result of dysfunction somewhere within the central cognitive system (i.e. 'central' in the sense of Fodor's 'central systems' (1983) — one might also refer to this type of dysfunction, therefore, as 'central pragmatic disability'). The cognitive dissociation of (at least some) linguistic abilities from central nonlinguistic abilities is now fairly widely accepted as a result of research into Williams syndrome (Bellugi, Marks, Bihrle and Sabo 1988) and cases like Yamada's Laura (Yamada 1990) and Smith and Tsimpli's 'linguist savant' (Smith and Tsimpli 1995) where precocious linguistic competence exists side by side with very low intelligence and other cognitive deficits. Although these are extreme examples and in many cases the relative contribution of linguistic and non-linguistic impairment may not be so easy to establish in practice (see the discussion of 'complex pragmatic disability' below), the distinction is still well worth making in principle. Further evidence for such a dissociation which is far more familiar to speech and language therapists can be found in cases of aphasia and other language disorders where relatively effective communication can still be achieved, in spite of impairment to the language system, through compensatory use of nonlinguistic cognitive abilites (e.g. Penn 1984; Perkins 1996). A list of the major cognitive systems which underlie primary pragmatic ability is given in Figure 1 and repeated as Figure 2.

inferential ability
social cognition
theory of mind
executive function
memory
affect
world knowledge

Figure 2. *Nonlinguistic cognitive systems which contribute to Primary Pragmatic Ability*

This list makes no claims about the modular status of each system, and indeed there is certainly considerable overlap between them (for example between theory of mind and social cognition on the one hand (Karmiloff-Smith, Klima, Bellugi, Grant and Baron-Cohen 1995), and between theory of mind and executive function on the other (Hughes, Russell and Robbins 1994)). It is offered simply as a checklist of cognitive abilities which, if impaired, are likely to result in the type of communicative impairment which I am labelling broadly as PPD. I will now give a brief outline of each system and show how its dysfunction may contribute to PPD.

4.1 *Inferential Ability*

Although some have argued that inferential reasoning is verbally mediated, neuropsychological evidence suggests that it may well be an independent cognitive process (Johnson-Laird 1995). Bishop and Adams (1992), for example, showed that children with specific language impairment (SLI) were impaired in constructing an integrated representation from a sequence of propositions even when these were presented nonverbally. Missing the point and drawing the wrong conclusion are commonly found in right brain damage (RBD) where language ability is intact and are evident in communicative behaviours such as failing to understand indirect requests, verbal irony and the punchlines of jokes (Molloy, Brownell and Gardner 1990). Similar difficulties with inference are also found in children with semantic-pragmatic disorder (Bishop and Adams 1989). In example (1) (from Perkins 1998), a child with a diagnosis of semantic-pragmatic disorder is unable to carry out a particularly obvious inference until relevant information is presented visually.

(1)   T (therapist) and P (child) are playing a picture guessing game
        T   this one is an animal
        P   oh
        T   and it barks - it goes woof woof
        P   oh dear
        T   what kind of animal is that?
        P   it's gonna run and run
        T   it's an animal - and it can run
        P   yes
        T   and it goes woof woof woof woof woof
        P   yes
        T   what kind of animal is it?
        P   a lion?
        T   a lion? it might be or it might be ...
        P   the lion - the lion
        T   *(shows picture)*
        P   a dog

The main problem for such children and for adults with RBD appears to be an inability to coordinate a sufficiently varied range of frames of reference, rather than being simply a deficit in the deductive process itself.

As well as playing a role in the instances of PPD described above, inference is also implicated in several of the other nonlinguistic cognitive systems discussed below.

4.2 *Social Cognition and Theory of Mind*

Social cognition is defined by McTear and Conti-Ramsden (1992) as the ability "to make social inferences about the actions, beliefs, and intentions of other persons in order to understand the behaviour of others and to be able to adapt messages to their needs" (p. 159). A 'theory of mind', defined by Carruthers and Smith (1996) as "the ability ... to explain and predict the actions, both of oneself, and of other intelligent agents", is an integral component of social cognition, as are the ability to turn-take and to modify others' behaviour through one's own actions. There is some debate regarding the modular integrity of social cognition (Karmiloff-Smith *et al.* 1995), though evidence is beginning to emerge for a neural correlate of theory of mind in the medial frontal gyrus on the left (Fletcher, Happé, Frith, Baker, Dolan, Frackowiak and Frith 1995). Deficits in social cognition are manifested in behaviours which range from an inability to predict precisely how much information to encode in one's utterances to satisfy an interlocutor's needs (as in the exchange in example (2) between a therapist and a child with semantic-pragmatic disorder), to an inability in full-blown autism to entertain the possibility that other people might have mental states such as beliefs, intentions and desires (Baron-Cohen, Leslie and Frith 1985).

(2)   Therapist   what will happen if he doesn't get better?
       Child   he - - get some medicine - and make - and make - -
                    my brother was feeling sick on Monday
       Therapist   right
       Child   - and I took my trouser off
       Therapist   uhuh - why did you take your trousers off?
       Child   he was sick on my trouser
       (from Bishop and Adams 1989)

4.3   *Executive Function*

Executive function is "an umbrella term for the mental operations which enable an individual to disengage from the immediate context in order to guide behaviour by reference to mental models or future goals" (Hughes *et al.* 1994: 477) and includes intentionality, planning, attention, flexibility and abstract reasoning. It therefore overlaps to some extent with other nonlinguistic systems. Ongoing research in the cognitive neurosciences should gradually clarify such overlap and the individual and conjoint contributions of its various components (Gazzaniga 1995). Executive dysfunction typically occurs as a result of damage to the frontal lobes and is seen as a key contributory factor to repetitiveness, poor topic maintenance and poor conversational performance generally in disorders such as schizophrenia (Morrison-Stewart, Williamson, Corning, Kutcher, Snow and Merskey 1992), autism (Frith and Happé 1994) and closed head injury (Perkins, Body and Parker 1995). The following extract is an example of poor topic maintenance in a man with closed head injury:

(3)   and did you 'know then what's 'happened to 'Colin ˇnow
        fallen off a `roof and fractured his ´skull you ˉknow that
        I look on life as a `bonus
        and just en'joy 'every `day as it `comes
        but . I would ˇsay . a 'bad fault of ˇmine
        and I would ˉsay s it's 'happening over t 'last - 'couple of ˇmonth
        I 'call a spade a ´spade a 'trump a ´trump
        and - I 'just said to `Sarah
        because I 'do go to `church a 'lot
        and I 'said she says 'what people do I `love
        and I says I only `love ´four
        (from Perkins *et al.* 1995: 296–7)

4.4 *Memory*

Memory has also been linked to the frontal lobes (Shimamura 1995) and overlaps to a considerable extent with executive function. It has been regarded as contributing to poor linguistic performance across a range of communication disorders including schizophrenia (Maher and Spitzer 1993), aphasia (Caplan and Waters 1995), SLI (Kushnir and Blake 1996), autism (Boucher and Lewis 1989) and closed head injury (Baddeley, Harris, Sunderland, Watts and Wilson 1987). As an example of how memory impairment may contribute to PPD, Perkins, Body and Parker (1996) suggest that excessive repetitiveness and topic bias in one particular case of closed head injury may be seen as a compensatory conversational strategy used to conceal the fact that the client has forgotten what has been, and is being, talked about by either switching to a favourite default topic or by providing a general statement of opinion.

4.5 *Affect*

Affect, or emotion, plays a key role in communication and is strongly linked to social cognition and theory of mind. The linguistic system that most directly expresses one's affective state is prosody, and it is important to distinguish between on the one hand cases of 'dysprosody' and 'prosodic disability' (Crystal 1981) where one lacks either the physical or linguistic means of prosodically expressing one's affective state, and on the other hand cases where the prosodic system itself is intact and atypical prosodic patterns are simply a reflection of an affective impairment and therefore an instance of PPD. Examples of the latter can be found in RBD (Ross 1988), autism (Fine, Bartolucci, Ginsberg and Szatmari 1991), Downs syndrome (Reilly, Klima and Bellugi 1990) and depression (Scherer 1986). Reilly *et al.* (1990) provide an interesting comparison between children with Downs syndrome, Williams syndrome and autism. In both, affect and linguistic ability are closely related, with the difference that Downs children perform poorly in both domains whereas Williams children perform exceptionally well, given their other cognitive deficits, and express affect through a range of prosodic and lexical devices. With autistic children, on the other hand, linguistic ability and affect appear to be dissociated. Autistic children have problems identifying the affective states of others (van Lancker, Cornelius and Needleman 1991) (which appears to be linked to an impaired theory of mind (Brothers and Ring 1992)) and although there is little evidence of a primary dysprosody or prosodic disability, the range of emotions they express is often communicatively inappropriate.

4.6 *World Knowledge*

Levelt (1989: 9–10) distinguishes between two different types of preverbal knowledge which must exist before the encoding of messages for communication may take place. The first is *procedural* knowledge, for example 'IF the intention is to commit oneself to the truth of p, THEN assert p' where p is some proposition the speaker wishes to express. The content of p is part of a store of *declarative* or *encyclopedic* knowledge built up over the speaker's lifetime and available in long-term memory. This will also include *situational* knowledge relating to the time, place, interlocutors and other features of the speaker's context of utterance, and a *discourse record* which keeps track of what has been said in the course of the interaction. World knowledge thus depends on other cognitive systems such as memory and social cognition for its storage and acquisition, and in addition is closely linked to the lexicon in which each lexical item is represented in terms of both its linguistic and conceptual characteristics. The state of one's world knowledge will depend on the effective functioning of other cognitive systems during its past development, and also during acts of language production and comprehension. There are several ways in which an individual's world knowledge may be atypical and therefore contributory towards PPD. Low intelligence or mental handicap can often lead to limited interests and therefore to a circumscribed knowledge base. This in turn contributes to conversational repetitiveness, a limited conversational range and topic bias (Rein and Kernan 1989). A similarly circumscribed knowledge base is also typical in autism as a result of obsessive interests (Baron-Cohen 1989). Because of their sociocognitive limitations, many aspects of social interaction are a closed book to people with autism, which further restricts what they are able to know. As Temple Grandin, a very able autistic person, notes: "My interests are factual and my recreational reading consists mostly of science and livestock publications. I have little interest in novels with complicated interpersonal relationships" (quoted in Sacks 1995: 249).

5.   Secondary Pragmatic Disability

There is a trivial sense in which *any* impairment might be labelled as an example of pragmatic disability insofar as it affects the use of language. Unfortunately, though, the pragmatic continuum extending from central to peripheral has not been charted in any systematic way. McTear and Conti-Ramsden (1992) show clearly that pragmatic disability is not a unitary phenomenon and illustrate a range of contributary factors such as linguistic, cognitive and social deficits. However, they stop short of providing any systematic means of classifying different varieties. But without a classificatory scheme, we have no means of drawing a line between pragmatic and non-pragmatic disability, or between conditions where the dysfunction in question contributes either directly or indirectly to problems with language use. I therefore propose to distinguish between Primary Pragmatic Disability, as defined and illustrated above, and *Secondary Pragmatic Disability* (SPD) which can be applied to instances of communicative impairment not due to nonlinguistic cognitive impairment. SPD can be a consequence of either linguistic dysfunction or sensorimotor dysfunction. I will briefly illustrate both.

5.1   *Linguistic Dysfunction*

Any speech or language disorder inevitably reduces communicative effectiveness, and there is therefore a sense in which a phonological, grammatical or semantic limitation can also be described as incurring a concomitant pragmatic disorder (i.e. SPD). In particular, a speaker impaired in this way is restricted in the range of choices available for encoding what they wish to say. SPD can result from impairment at any language level.

5.1.1 *Syntax and Morphology*
The extract of conversation in example (4), spoken by a 51 year old man, is typical of language performance in nonfluent aphasia.

(4)   oh it's alright aye . mate . mate . Jack comes and all but . . er . oh
        dear . Jack . . er . old er . . seventy . no . sixty eight . Jack . . but
        swim . me . me like this . . swimming . . er . . I can't say it . . but
        Jack . . er . . swimming on front . er . . back
        (from Perkins and Varley, 1996)

We can tell that he is trying to say something about himself and his mate Jack
who is sixty-eight, and either or both of them swimming either on their front or
back, but his problems with inflectional morphology, syntax and some difficulties with lexical access reduce the choices for encoding sufficient information for
the speaker to arrive at an unambiguous interpretation. His communicative
effectiveness is thus impaired and this can therefore be described as an instance
of SPD. It also, incidentally, constitutes a pragmatic problem for the hearer who
is obliged to contribute an atypical amount of inferential effort to retrieve the
intended meaning (Perkins 1996).

5.1.2 Lexis
The extract in example (5), spoken by a 56 year old woman with fluent aphasia,
shows a somewhat different picture.

(5)   if we can just . see . we can . I can . I can . I can read . normally .
        but when I can't it's hazy . it goes faded and then I say go on . go
        on . go on then . and they just say it and I say it . but er it's here
        [points to head]
        (from Perkins and Varley, 1996)

The difficulty for the hearer in working out what she is trying to say lies in her
excessive use of the pronominal *it* instead of a less referentially opaque nominal
form. Although her syntax and morphology appear to be largely intact, she is unable
to encode sufficient information lexically, which once again reduces her communicative effectiveness and places a heavy inferential processing load on the hearer.

5.1.3 Segmental Phonology
Phonological impairment typically leads to excessive homophony. One 4 year old
child, who was unable to produce velars, voiceless plosives, syllable-final
plosives and consonant clusters, realized each of the target forms 'cat', 'grass'
and 'clap' as [dæ]. Although the child's phonology was internally consistent, its
underspecification required inferential compensation from the hearer.

5.1.4 Prosody
Prosody can also be reduced and underspecified compared with the normal adult

target. One 4 year old boy, described in Perkins (1985), was extremely restricted in his deployment of intonation and contrastive stress. All of his syllables were fully stressed, and his only tone, a long low-to-high rise, was always placed on the final syllable of an utterance. Although this prosodic pattern was sometimes accidentally appropriate, its lack of variability meant that any contrastivity and attitudinal meaning of the type usually conveyed prosodically had to be inferred independently, and this severely reduced his communicative effectiveness.

In each of the above examples of SPD, the primary deficit is a linguistic one but can be seen as entailing a concomitant or secondary pragmatic problem.

5.2 *Sensorimotor Dysfunction*

As well as being directly affected by central and linguistic cognitive capacity, communicative effectiveness is also partly dependent upon sensory input systems such as auditory and visual perception and motor output systems which govern the movements of the vocal tract, gesture, posture and facial expression. It may initially appear slightly odd to include such phenomena in a discussion of pragmatic disability, but if we regard pragmatic functioning as a *consequence* of interactions between cognitive systems, rather than as a primary cognitive system in its own right, then sensory and motor systems play an equally key role to those of central and linguistic systems in that they permit a range of choices for the encoding and decoding of communicative behaviour, and their dysfunction can seriously reduce the effectiveness of such behaviour by limiting the available choices. There are a range of sensorimotor disorders which may impair communication and may therefore be seen as contributing to SPD. I will briefly mention just a few for purposes of illustration.

5.2.1 *Hearing impairment*
Hearing impairment influences overall communicative performance in numerous ways. Mogford-Bevan (1993) reviews, for example, how difficulties in hearing others and being heard themselves affect the conversational performance of hearing-impaired children — e.g. shorter conversational turns and fewer initiations, as well as that of their interlocutors — e.g. imposing a higher degree of control.

5.2.2 *Visual impairment*
Visual handicap has a similarly wide range of consequences for communicative performance. Mills (1993) reports that turntaking patterns of blind adults are different from those of sighted adults, and that adults talking to blind children initiate topics more than when talking to sighted children. Young blind children also

tend to imitate interlocutors' utterances more than sighted children and use more formulaic language (Perez-Pereira 1994).

5.2.3 *Motor impairment*
An inability to effect a full range of physical movement, whether for organic or neurological reasons, can severely impair communicative ability. Motor impairment can range from the fairly general and pervasive as in cerebral palsy and Parkinson's disease, to more specific loss of movement due to selective paralysis of limbs, face or vocal tract, each of which has important consequences for communicative behaviour (Ramig 1992). Where the vocal organs are involved, motor or neuromuscular deficits may result in dyspraxia or dysarthria, with potentially severe communicative consequences. Similarly, articulatory impairment resulting from anatomical defects such as cleft palate may also severely affect a speaker's ability to communicate effectively (Howard 1993).

6.   Complex Pragmatic Disability

There may be different subtypes, or degrees, of CPD. In the example of lexical underspecification in autism above, the linguistic deficit is an ontogenetic consequence of sociocognitive impairment. Another possible example of this is specific language impairment (SLI), in that there is recent evidence to suggest that the linguistic deficits found in children with SLI are linked both to problems with sequential verbal memory (e.g. Kushnir and Blake 1996) and auditory perception (Fletcher and Ingham 1995). In acquired disorders, on the other hand, linguistic deficit may result from an on-line cognitive processing deficit. Kolk (1995), for example, argues that agrammatism in aphasia is caused by problems with timing and coordination during syntactic processing. In other words, grammatical competence may be intact but cannot be successfully deployed because of disruption in other cognitive systems. A further type of CPD can arise as a result of compensatory communicative strategies (Perkins 1996). People with aphasia often employ a range of such strategies to enhance their communicative effectiveness (Penn 1984), but sometimes there can be unintended negative consequences. For example, receptive aphasics will often try to hold on to their conversational turn in order to reduce the number of occasions where they might misundersand what their interlocutors say to them. Sometimes this might be perceived as an instance of PPD (e.g. sociocognitive deficit) rather than SPD (i.e. linguistic deficit). Finally, there are, of course, cases where both a linguistic and a nonlinguistic deficit exist simultaneously but unconnectedly. It might be more accurate to describe these in terms of 'compound' rather than 'complex' pragmatic disability. In practice, many cases of pragmatic disability commonly encountered may well be complex in the way described here. Ultimately, though, our ability to distinguish between CPD on the one hand, and PPD and/or SPD on the other, will depend on how well we understand the disorders in question, and the effectiveness of the assessment tools available to us.

7. Conclusion

The classificatory system presented in this chapter and summarised in Figure 3 is a reaction to the fact that the term 'pragmatic disability' is too broad and vague to be of much use in the diagnosis and remediation of communicative impairments. The scheme is based on a distinction between a) the behavioural symptoms of communicative dysfunction, and b) the cognitive, linguistic and sensorimotor impairments which cause them. The widespread use of the term 'pragmatic disability' to refer indiscriminately to both of these has resulted in considerable confusion, particularly in the case of certain communication disorders which, despite being similar in their surface manifestations, are aetiologically quite distinct. A strong implication of this approach for clinical practice is that instead of focusing exclusively on the linguistic behaviours identified by pragmatic theory, therapy should be directed at the underlying causes. For example, rather than simply noting whether a patient may be described as having problems with Grice's maxim of quantity or with indirect speech acts, we should in addition be trying to ascertain whether this is a result of, say, a sociocognitive deficit (PPD), a problem with sentence formulation or visuo-spatial perception (SPD) or some combination of both (CPD).

Type of pragmatic disability	Underlying cause
Primary Pragmatic Disability (PPD)	*Dysfunction of:* inferential ability; social cognition; theory of mind; executive function; memory; affect; world knowledge
Secondary Pragmatic Disability (SPD)	*a) Linguistic dysfunction*, i.e.: syntax, morphology, phonology, prosody, lexis
	b) Sensorimotor dysfunction, i.e.: auditory perception; visual perception; motor ability
Complex Pragmatic Disability (CPD)	*Combination of PPD and SPD*

Figure 3. *Classification of pragmatic disability*

Notes

1. For example, if one adopts rather loose definitions such as 'pragmatics = contextualised language use' and 'discourse = a sequence of utterances' then part of the context of language use will consist of preceding and following utterances (i.e. pragmatics includes discourse), and the coherence of a given sequence of utterances will be partly determined by their context of use (i.e. discourse includes pragmatics).

2. There is, however, a fairly extensive literature which makes use of discourse analysis techniques to examine narrative ability in communication-impaired children (see, for example, Hudson and Murdoch, 1992; Liles, 1993; Dennis, Jacennik and Barnes, 1994)

3. In discussions of pragmatics, the notion of 'module' is not always consistently represented. I will assume here a broadly Fodorean definition (Fodor, 1983) — i.e. that a module is domain specific, informationally encapsulated, fast, possesses a dedicated neural architecture and manifests characteristic patterns of breakdown. Craig's (1995) use of the term bears only a loose resemblance to that of Fodor. Kasher's (1991) modified version is somewhat closer to Fodor's. In the account presented here I will often avoid explicit reference to the debate on the modularity of mind and simply refer generally to cognitive 'systems'. For further discussion of the status of such cognitive systems, see Perkins (1998).

4. For similar criticisms of this term, see McTear and Conti-Ramsden (1992) and Smith and Leinonen (1992).

References

Ahlsén, E. 1993. "Conversational principles and aphasic communication". *Journal of Pragmatics* 19: 57–70.

Armstrong, E. M. 1991. "The potential of cohesion analysis in the analysis and treatment of aphasic discourse". *Clinical Linguistics and Phonetics* 5: 39–51.

Baddeley, A., Harris, J., Sunderland, A., Watts, K. P. and Wilson, B. 1987. "Closed head injury and memory". In *Neurobehavioral Recovery from Head Injury*, H. S. Levin, J. Grafman and H. M. Eisenberg (eds), 295–317. Oxford: Oxford University Press.

Baron-Cohen, S. 1989. "Do autistic children have obsessions and compulsions?". *British Journal of Clinical Psychology* 28: 193–200.

Baron-Cohen, S., Leslie, A. M. and Frith, U. 1985. "Does the autistic child have a 'theory of mind'?". *Cognition* 21: 37–46.

Bellugi, U., Marks, S., Bihrle, A. and Sabo, H. 1988. "Dissociation between language and cognitive functions in Williams syndrome". In *Language Development in Exceptional Circumstances*, D. V. M. Bishop and K. Mogford (eds), 177–189. London: Churchill Livingstone.

Bishop, D. V. M. and Adams, C. 1989. "Conversational characteristics of children with semantic-pragmatic disorder. II: What features lead to a judgement of inappropriacy?". *British Journal of Disorders of Communication* 24: 241–263.

Bishop, D. V. M. and Adams, C. 1992. "Comprehension problems in children with specific language impairment — literal and inferential meaning". *Journal of Speech and Hearing Research* 35: 119–129.

Bloom, R. L., Obler, L. K., De Santi, S. and Ehrlich, J. S. (eds) 1994. *Discourse Analysis and Applications: Studies in Adult Clinical Populations.* Hillsdale, NJ: Erlbaum.

Boucher, J. and Lewis, V. 1989. "Memory impairments and communication in relatively able autistic children". *Journal of Child Psychology and Psychiatry* 30: 99–122.

Brothers, L. and Ring, B. 1992. "A neuroethological framework for the representation of minds". *Journal of Cognitive Neuroscience* 4: 107–118.

Caplan, D. and Waters, G. S. 1995. "Aphasic disorders of syntactic comprehension and working memory capacity". *Cognitive Neuropsychology* 12: 637–649.

Carruthers, P. and Smith, P. K. 1996. "Introduction". In *Theories of Theories of Mind*, P. Carruthers and P. K. Smith (eds), 1–8. Cambridge: Cambridge University Press.

Chapman, S. B. and Ulatowska, H. K. 1989 "Discourse in aphasia: integration deficits in processing reference". *Brain and Language* 36: 651–669.

Craig, H. K. 1995. Pragmatic impairments. In *The Handbook of Child Language*, P. Fletcher and B. MacWhinney (eds), 623–640. Oxford: Blackwell.

Crystal, D. 1981. *Clinical Linguistics*. London: Whurr.

Damico, J. S. 1985. "Clinical discourse analysis: A functional approach to language assessment". In *Communication Skills and Classroom Success*, C. S. Simon (ed), 165–204. Basingstoke: Taylor and Francis.

Dennis, M., Jacennik, B. and Barnes, M. A. 1994. "The content of narrative discourse in children and adolescents after early-onset hydrocephalus and in normally developing age peers." *Brain and Language* 46: 129–165.

Ferguson, A. 1996. "Describing competence in aphasic/normal conversation". *Clinical Linguistics and Phonetics* 10: 55–63.

Fine, J., Bartolucci, G., Ginsberg, G. and Szatmari, P. 1991. "The use of intonation to communicate in pervasive developmental disorders". *Journal of Child Psychology and Psychiatry* 32: 771–782.

Fletcher, P. and Ingham, R. 1995. Grammatical impairment. In *The Handbook of Child Language*, P. Fletcher and B. MacWhinney (eds), 603–622. Oxford: Blackwell.

Fletcher, P. C., Happé, F., Frith, U., Baker, S. C., Dolan, R. J., Frackowiak, R. S. J. and Frith, C. D. 1995. "Other minds in the brain: a functional imaging study of 'theory of mind' in story comprehension". *Cognition* 57: 109–128.

Fodor, J. A. 1983. *The Modularity of Mind: An Essay on Faculty Psychology*. Cambridge, Mass: MIT Press.

Frith, U. 1989. *Autism: Explaining the Enigma*. Oxford: Blackwell.

Frith, U. and Happé, F. 1994. "Autism: Beyond 'theory of mind'". *Cognition* 50: 115–132.

Gallagher, T. M. (ed) 1991. *Pragmatics of Language: Clinical Practice Issues*. London: Chapman and Hall.

Gazzaniga, M. S. (ed) 1995. *The Cognitive Neurosciences*. Cambridge, Mass: MIT Press.

Happé, F. G. E. 1991. "The autobiographical writings of three Asperger syndrome adults: Problems of interpretation and implications for theory". In *Autism and Asperger Syndrome*, U. Frith (ed), 207–242. Cambridge: Cambridge University Press.

Happé, F. G. E. 1993. "Communicative competence and theory of mind in autism: A test of relevance theory." *Cognition* 48: 101–119.

Hirst, W., LeDoux, J. and Stein, S. 1984. "Constraints on the processing of indirect speech acts: Evidence from aphasiology". *Brain and Language* 23: 26–33.

Horn, L. R. 1988. "Pragmatic theory". In *Linguistics: The Cambridge Survey. I: Linguistic Theory: Foundations*, F. J. Newmeyer (ed), 113–145. Cambridge: Cambridge University Press.

Howard, S. J. 1993. "Articulatory constraints on a phonological system: a case study of cleft palate speech". *Clinical Linguistics and Phonetics* 7: 299–317.

Hudson, L. J. and Murdoch, B. E. 1992. "Spontaneously generated narratives of children treated for posterior fossa tumour". *Aphasiology* 6: 549–566.

Hughes, C., Russell, J. and Robbins, T. W. 1994. "Evidence for executive dysfunction in autism". *Neuropsychologia* 32: 477–492.

Joanette, Y. and Brownell, H. H. (eds) 1990. *Discourse Ability and Brain Damage: Theoretical and Empirical Perspectives*. New York: Springer-Verlag.

Johnson-Laird, P. N. 1995. "Mental models, deductive reasoning, and the brain". In *The Cognitive Neurosciences*, M. S. Gazzaniga (ed), 999–1008. Cambridge, Mass: MIT Press.

Karmiloff-Smith, A., Klima, E., Bellugi, U., Grant, J. and Baron-Cohen, S. 1995. "Is there a social module? Language, face processing, and theory of mind in individuals with Williams syndrome". *Journal of Cognitive Neuroscience* 7: 196–208.

Kasher, A. 1991. "On the pragmatic modules: a lecture". *Journal of Pragmatics* 16: 381–397.

Kasher, A. 1994. "Modular pragmatics". In *The Encyclopedia of Language and Linguistics*, R. E. Asher (ed), 3279–3280. Oxford: Pergamon.

Kolk, H. 1995. "A time-based approach to agrammatic production". *Brain and Language* 50: 282–303.

Kushnir, C. C. and Blake, J. 1996. "The nature of the cognitive deficit in specific language impairment". *First Language* 16: 21–40.

Levelt, W. J. M. 1989: *Speaking: From Intention to Articulation*. Cambridge, Mass.: MIT Press.

Levinson, S. C. 1983. *Pragmatics*. Cambridge: Cambridge University Press.

Liles, B. Z. 1993. "Narrative discourse in children with language disorders and children with normal language: a critical review of the literature". *Journal of Speech and Hearing Research* 36: 868–882.

Local, J. and Wootton, T. 1995. "Interactional and phonetic aspects of immediate echolalia in autism: a case study". *Clinical Linguistics and Phonetics* 9: 155–184.

Loveland, K. A., Landry, S. H., Hughes, S. O., Hall, S. K. and McEvoy, R. 1988. "Speech acts and the pragmatic deficits of autism". *Journal of Speech and Hearing Research* 31: 593–604.

Lucas, E. V. 1980. *Semantic and Pragmatic Language Disorders*. Aspen Systems.

Maher, B. A. and Spitzer, M. 1993. "Thought disorders and language behavior in schizophrenia". In *Linguistic Disorders and Pathologies: An International Handbook*, G. Blanken, J. Dittmann, H. Grimm, J. C. Marshall and C.-W. Wallesch (eds), 522–533. Berlin: Walter de Gruyter.

McDonald, S. 1992. "Differential pragmatic language loss after closed head injury: ability to comprehend conversational implicature". *Applied Psycholinguistics* 13: 295–312.

McTear, M. F. and Conti-Ramsden, G. 1992. *Pragmatic Disability in Children*. London: Whurr.

Mills, A. E. 1993. "Language acquisition and development with sensory impairment: blind children". In *Linguistic Disorders and Pathologies: An International Handbook*, G. Blanken, J. Dittmann, H. Grimm, J. C. Marshall and C.-W. Wallesch (eds), 679–687. Berlin: Walter de Gruyter.

Mogford-Bevan, K. 1993. "Language acquisition and development with sensory impairment: hearing-impaired children". In *Linguistic Disorders and Pathologies: An International Handbook*, G. Blanken, J. Dittmann, H. Grimm, J. C. Marshall and C.-W. Wallesch (eds), 660–679. Berlin: Walter de Gruyter.

Molloy, R., Brownell, H. H. and Gardner, H. 1990. "Discourse comprehension by right-hemisphere stroke patients: deficits of prediction and revision". In *Discourse Ability and Brain Damage: Theoretical and Empirical* Perspectives, Y. Joanette and H. H. Brownell (eds), 113–130. New York: Springer-Verlag.

Morris, J. and Franklin, S. 1995. "Aphasia: assessment and remediation of a speech discrimination deficit". In *Case Studies in Clinical Linguistics*, M. R. Perkins and S. J. Howard (eds), 245–270. London: Whurr.

Morrison-Stewart, S. L., Williamson, P. C., Corning, W. C., Kutcher, S. P., Snow, W. G. and Merskey, H. 1992. "Frontal and non-frontal lobe neuropsychological test performance and clinical symptomatology in schizophrenia". *Psychological Medicine* 22: 353–359.

Penn, C. 1984. "Compensatory strategies in aphasia: behavioural and neurological correlates". In *Neuropsychology II*, K. W. Grieve and R. D. Griesel (eds). Pretoria: Monicol.

Penn, C. 1985. "The profile of communicative appropriateness". *The South African Journal of Communication Disorders* 32: 18–23.

Penn, C. 1988. "The profiling of syntax and pragmatics in aphasia". *Clinical Linguistics and Phonetics* 2: 179–208.

Perez-Pereira, M. 1994. "Imitations, repetitions, routines, and the child's analysis of language: insights from the blind". *Journal of Child Language* 21: 317–338.

Perkins, M. R. 1985. "Discourse error analysis". In *Papers from the First Leeds English Language Teaching Symposium*, P. Roach (ed), 4–8. Leeds: Leeds University.

Perkins, M. R. 1996. "The compensations of an unbalanced mind: a cognitive-interactive account of disorders of language and thought". *Paper presented at the Hang Seng Conference on Language and Thought, University of Sheffield*.

Perkins, M. R. 1998. "Is pragmatics epiphenomenal?: evidence from communication disorders". *Journal of Pragmatics* 29: 291–311.

Perkins, M. R., Body, R. and Parker, M. 1995. "Closed head injury: assessment and remediation of topic bias and repetitiveness". In *Case Studies in Clinical Linguistics*, M. R. Perkins and S. J. Howard (eds), 293–320. London: Whurr.

Perkins, M. R., Body, R. and Parker, M. 1996. "Topic management in closed head injury". In *Pathologies of Speech and language: Contributions of Clinical Phonetics and Linguistics*, T. W. Powell (ed), 89–94. New Orleans, LA: ICPLA.

Perkins, M. R. and Varley, R. 1996. *A Machine-Readable Corpus of Aphasic Discourse*. University of Sheffield: Department of Human Communication Sciences/Institute for Language, Speech and Hearing (ILASH).

Prutting, C. A. and Kirchner, D. M. 1983. "Applied pragmatics". In *Pragmatic Assessment and Intervention Issues in Language*, T. M. Gallagher and C. A. Prutting (eds), 29–64. San Diego: College Hill Press.

Prutting, C. A. and Kirchner, D. M. 1987. "A clinical appraisal of the pragmatic aspects of language". *Journal of Speech and Hearing Disorders* 52: 105–119.

Ramig, L. O. 1992. "The role of phonation in speech intelligibility: a review and preliminary data from patients with Parkinson's disease". In *Intelligibility in Speech Disorders: Theory, Measurement and Management*, R. D. Kent (ed), 119–155. Amsterdam: John Benjamins.

Rapin, I. and Allen, D. A. 1983. "Developmental language disorders: Nosologic considerations". In *Neuropsychology of Language, Reading, and Spelling*, U. Kirk (ed), 155–184. New York: Academic Press.

Reilly, J., Klima, E. S. and Bellugi, U. 1990. "Once more with feeling: affect and language in atypical populations". *Development and Psychopathology* 2: 367–391.

Rein, R. P. and Kernan, K. T. 1989. "The functional use of verbal perseverations by adults who are mentally retarded". *Education and Training in Mental Retardation* 24: 381–389.

Ripich, D. N. and Terrell, B. Y. 1988. "Patterns of discourse cohesion and coherence in Alzheimer's Disease". *Journal of Speech and Hearing Disorders* 53: 8–15.

Ross, E. D. 1988. "Language-related functions of the right cerebral hemisphere". In *Aphasia*, F. C. Rose, R. Whurr and M. A. Wyke (eds), 188–209. London: Whurr.

Roth, F. P. and Spekman, N. J. 1984. "Assessing the pragmatic abilities of children: Part 1. Organizational framework and assessment parameters". *Journal of Speech and Hearing Disorders* 49: 2–11.

Sacks, O. 1995. *An Anthropologist on Mars: Seven Paradoxical Tales*. London: Picador.

Scherer, K. R. 1986. "Vocal affect expression: a review and a model for future research". *Psychological Bulletin* 99: 143–165.

Shimamura, A. P. 1995. "Memory and frontal lobe function." In *The Cognitive Neurosciences*, M. S. Gazzaniga (ed), 803–813. Cambridge, Mass: MIT Press.

Smith, B. R. and Leinonen, E. 1992. *Clinical Pragmatics: Unravelling the Complexities of Communicative Failure*. London: Chapman and Hall.

Smith, N. V. and Tsimpli, I.-M. 1995. *The Mind of a Savant: Language-Learning and Modularity*. Oxford: Blackwell.

Van Lancker, D., Cornelius, C. and Needleman, R. 1991. "Comprehension of verbal terms for emotions in normal, autistic, and schizophrenic children". *Developmental Neuropsychology* 7: 1–18.

Willcox, A. and Mogford-Bevan, K. 1995. "Conversational disability: assessment and remediation". In *Case Studies in Clinical Linguistics*. M. R. Perkins and S. J. Howard (eds), 146–178. London: Whurr.

Wilson, D. and Sperber, D. 1991. "Pragmatics and modularity". In *Pragmatics: A Reader*, S. Davis (ed), 583–595. Oxford: Oxford University Press. (First published in *The Chicago Linguistic Society Parasession on Pragmatics and Grammatical Theory*, A. M. Farley, P. T. Farley and K.-E. McCullough (eds), 1986. Chicago: The Chicago Linguistic Society).

Wykes, T. and Leff, J. 1982. "Disordered speech: Differences between manics and schizophrenics". *Brain and Language* 15: 117–124.

Yamada, J. 1990. *Laura: A Case for the Modularity of Language*. Cambridge, MA: MIT Press.

What Do You Have in Mind?

Beliefs Knowledge and Pragmatic Impairment

John Wilson
University of Ulster

Lorraine McAnulty
*Down Lisburn Health and
Social Services Trust*

1. Introduction

In this paper we will focus on one particular aspect of pragmatic impairment as revealed in conversational interaction. This impairment combines difficulties in referential behaviour with an inability to take account of an other's knowledge in providing relevant topic responses. Our main example is drawn from recorded therapeutic interactions involving children defined by their therapists as having a semantic-pragmatic language disorder (SPLD). The designation of these children as semantic-pragmatic disordered is based on a clinical diagnosis following Rapin and Allen (1983), who introduced the term semantic-pragmatic language disorder. While it is accepted that the children designated by their clinicians as SPLD clearly suffer from a form of conversational disability, we are not completely comfortable with the term semantic-pragmatic language disorder. This is not necessarily a criticism, since it reflects the reality of a transient phase between a growing interest in children suffering from difficulties in what we might broadly term conversational interaction, and our ability as analysts to theoretically articulate a clear account of both the location and structural nature of the disorder (see McTear and Conti-Ramsden 1992; also Perkins, this volume, on whether some problems are language based at all). Rapin and Allen's attempt to classify and label is understandable but unfortunate. A semantic-pragmatic disorder implies there are semantic disorders, pragmatic disorders, and some hybrid form of semantic-pragmatic disorders. In the present state of our knowledge, certainly of a relatively new and expanding field such as pragmatics, there is a need to carefully consider our ability to discern the individual location of semantic or pragmatic difficulties. It is here we should begin. After all, any location of difficulty or disorder will, in part, be driven by existing or emerging theories of language (and perhaps mind) at different levels, or in relation to form/function mappings. We are not aware of any core semantic-pragmatic theory; although we are aware of semantic theories and pragmatic theories, and various attempts to indicate and clarify the borders of semantic and pragmatic knowledge (see for example Sperber and Wilson 1996). For us then, and following Craig (1995), we prefer to use the term 'pragmatic impairment' to refer to levels of conversational disability.

Conversational disability comes in many forms but, in general, research indicates that at a broad level of pragmatic 'competency' an understanding of the underlying principles of producing *turns, acts, questions, requests* etc. seems relatively sound (see for example, Leonard, Camarata, Rowan and Chapman 1982; Leonard 1986; Leslie 1987; Van Kleeck and Frankel 1981; McTear and Conti-Ramsdem 1992). For this reason analysts have sometimes reflected on whether the problem these children display is not more social and cognitive than linguistic (Perkins, this volume). As Smith and Leinonen (1992) suggest: "what presents itself as a pragmatic disorder may in fact stem from some other type of underlying problem". Stubbs (1986) has also argued that the surface symptoms exhibited by children with so-called pragmatic impairments may reveal features indicative of a higher cognitive disorder, i.e. problems in reasoning and thinking. One result of these concerns has been to turn to a more functional view of the issues, or a 'performance' based model in Craig's (1995) terms. Here there is an assumption that there is a learning process involving form-function mappings, operating perhaps within a competition model of language which produces probabilistic settings based on acquired weightings (see Bates, Thal and MacWhinney 1991; cited in Craig 1995). But another reaction, and one we would support, is to see the link between language and higher cognitive disorders of thinking and reasoning as a natural one. Pragmatics explicitly relates language and cognition. Indeed, one recent and influential theory of pragmatics, Relevance Theory (Sperber and Wilson 1996), is presented unequivocally as a cognitive view of communication. In this spirit, the approach adopted in this paper is to view pragmatic impairment as residing at the cognitive/communication interface, and we argue that the children referred to in this study may be suffering from an inability to map social cognitive requirements for mutual/shared knowledge monitoring onto the production and maintenance mechanisms for topic coherence and construction.

In order to explain the difficulty faced by children suffering from this type of pragmatic impairment, we will combine Baron-Cohen's (1995) 'theory of the mind' model (built in part from an original formulation found in Leslie 1994), with Ballim and Wilks's (1992) model of 'artificial believers'. Baron-Cohen's model of the theory of the mind has been developed, in general, to explain, in evolutionary terms, the ability human beings have to take account of each other's views and representations of a shared world. In a similar way Ballim and Wilks (1992) have developed a formal artificial intelligence model of how systems (humans?) may represent not only their own beliefs and but also others' beliefs. We want to make use of the Ballim and Wilks (1992) view of beliefs as a formal way of representing some of the issues raised in a theory of the mind model of the type articulated by Baron-Cohen. The link of all this to the issue of pragmatic impairment as considered in this paper will be explored in detail below, but in general there are two reasons for considering these theories as a way of understanding specific aspects of pragmatic impairment. First, children suffering from what we are calling pragmatic impairments (and what Rapin and Allen 1983 call SPLD) have been directly compared to 'verbal autistic' children (see Rapin and Allen 1987), and such children, it has been claimed, suffer from a deficit of the theory of the mind. Second, the main focus of impairment in this chapter is on referential and topic construction difficulties, and both require speaker/hearers to take account of each other's knowledge/beliefs for reference and topic construction to succeed.

2. Reference, Coherence and Topic

Consider the following example:

1. T: Tell me this could you tell me a bit about what you were doing when I went into your class?
2. P: We were watching the Dragon's Eyes see the a/a Pheton exploded and (1 sec)
3. T: What's that what's a Pheton?
4. P: Phetacore/it was the energy of Pellamar
5. T: Right
6. P: and they had to go and find three Phetons/twenty theres only twenty five/there had to be twenty five bits of the Pheton phetacore and now three (.) were left (.) three were missing
7. T: Right and did they find them?
8: C: Yeh
9: T: Right
10: C: And then they got the Phetacore biting again

This example reveals all the elements of the core issues we want to explore. It is important to note that this is the opening of an interaction where the therapist (T) has no direct knowledge of what was explicitly taking place in the child's (P) classroom. Turn (1.) is a genuine request for information (as opposed to a test question frequently found in both clinic and classroom). In this context P is introducing a reference for a direct topic (the dragon's eyes) which T is unable to bring into focus. T attempts to make this clear, to some extent, at (3.). P's response at (4.) acts in a similar way to turn (2.) by providing reference items (Phetacore/the energy of Pellamar) which form part of the topic at (2.). However, since T cannot access the topic as a whole it would be equally impossible for her to access sub units of the topic at this point in the interaction (although she could work out structurally and sequentially that the response (4.) was related to the original topic; Sacks *et al.* 1975). Basically, then, P is attempting to construct a topic area for joint attention when the 'context' of the topic is not available to the listener. At turns (6.) and (10.) P makes use of referential pronominal forms such as 'they' and 'them' but without, that is, any prior accessing of relevant referential entities to which the listener may tag the pronominal markers. Two points then. First, the child has failed to adequately take account of relevant knowledge in the construction of topic. Second, the child is making anaphoric use of pronominal forms without first assuring, in Ariel's (1990) terms, that adequate *accessibility* marking has taken place (see below).

In observing nine children diagnosed in the same manner as Child A, all have revealed these same problems, to a greater or lesser extent (see McAnulty 1996). It is not the quantitative distribution of such forms that is important for these children, since only one occurrence of the type outlined above may lead to communication breakdown (although it is true that frequency of use may reflect severity of difficulty). In this sense we will concentrate our remarks around the example Child A has set, and using topic and referential problems as a starting point attempt to model such difficulties in a socio-cognitive framework which explains this type of pragmatic impairment. This modelling offers a level of explanation for the problem the child displays, but does not directly indicate how therapy might then proceed. An essential problem for any therapy, of course, is knowing what the problem is and in the case of pragmatic impairments it is important that we have some more detailed discussions of where potential problems might reside, only then will we be in a position to move forward in terms of therapeutic choices. In the last section of this chapter we will offer some observations on this very point. Following the modelling of an explanation of child A's problem we turn our attention briefly to the issue of therapy itself, and make some suggestions on how the often abstract and formal arguments found below may be utilised in the clinical context.

3. A Model of Mind Reading

Reference and topic construction are not, of course, mutually exclusive, and both have received, in their own way, a significant amount of attention within pragmatics. Topics have been explored in structural, sequential, psychological, and information processing terms (see Danes 1974; Kintsch and Van Dijk 1978; Johnson-Laird 1983; Schank and Abelson 1977). Equally, reference has received attention from many different perspectives from philosophy through linguistics and psychology to artificial intelligence (Clark and Wilkes-Gibbs 1986; Bilgrami 1996; Ariel 1990; Recanati 1993; Sacks and Schegloff 1979). For our purposes, however, we will operate with a relatively common sense view of both. We will refer to topic as the information context mutually constructed for the progress of talk within a sequentially defined frame. This means simply that on an entry into a topic, sequential elements of location come into play, i.e. the topic must begin somewhere and end somewhere; it must be introduced and it must be followed up (see Wilson 1989: ch. 3). The topic, however, is an informational frame (in the sense of Minsky 1975), around which both speaker and hearer operate. This frame may not be exactly the same for both speaker and hearer but there must be a level of shared access to allow talk to progress, or for the topic to develop.

Reference marks out objects and concepts in differing ways so that they may be brought into focus/mind or maintained within an emerging description, story, account or whatever (see for example the work of Clark and Wilkes-Gibbs 1986; Schober and Clark 1989). This may be achieved either directly through physical location, or indirectly through inference or reflection. In either case, however, a central feature of the use of reference and topic construction is on-line access and negotiation of elements either in the world or in the mind of both speaker and hearer, and for us this is the central issue.

Clearly, Child A has a problem in both reference and topic construction, at least in the example given above. But what would that problem be? One thing hinted at in the last paragraph is the cognitive orientation and manipulation of shared elements required in both topic construction and reference assignment. There has to be some level of agreement that participants are operating within the same frame, and that selected referential forms have been appropriately chosen at the appropriate time to both separate and maintain focus on relevant objects and individuals.

Taking the above comments as a starting point we want to approach A's problems by considering Baron-Cohen's view of what he calls 'mindreading.' We want to think about whether children who have difficulty providing correct reference or topic constraints suffer from an inability to construct what Baron-Cohen calls 'the shared attention mechanism', or whether, in a broader, and more fundamental sense, they suffer at the level of what has been termed the theory of the mind itself; perhaps constructing the beliefs of others as if they were their own beliefs.

Baron-Cohen (1995) has suggested that in evolutionary terms human beings have developed a 'mindreading system' which allows them to make sense of their own and others' behaviour. Most significant from our point of view is his claim that such a system is central to communication itself. He notes that questions such as 'What does he mean?' boil down to 'What does he intend me to understand'. There is a similarity here between this claim and classic communication theory which saw the sending and receiving of messages as the transference of thoughts from one mind to another. Baron-Cohen recognises, along with Sperber and Wilson (1996; see also Bach 1994), that such a view is incomplete in that we do not simply use language as a means of transferring the speaker's thought into the hearer's mind. Meaning is negotiated through a series of general principles which supplement and enrich simple propositions with elements from context, shared and mutual knowledge, and relevant social facts. Central to the process, however, is the fact that one only sends a message, of whatever kind, because one has intentionality (see Searle 1983) and believes others have the same. A fundamental principle of 'mindreading' and recognised in pragmatic theories in general (see specifically Sperber and Wilson 1996), is that of achieving some form of joint and monitored attention which focuses on listener needs as they operate in specific contexts. The development of such a process may be understood in terms of Baron-Cohen's model of *mindreading* as displayed in Figure 1.

The ID system is a basic form of intentionality detection; i.e. basic actions, such as moving forward or picking up an object, are goal driven pursuits in which agents engage in order to achieve specific ends. This is the basic level of mindreading, and the first level of understanding available to children. Explanations of how the world operates impute intentions, even when the objects themselves do not have human form. Heider and Simmel (1944: cf. Baron-Cohen 1995) provided evidence that when children were shown a silent film of geometric objects moving around, and then asked to describe these movements that they frequently did so by imputing agentive and intentional goals (he wants to get to X; they would only do that for Y). The evidence here suggests the fundamental need to understand the world in terms of the intention driven behaviour of others.

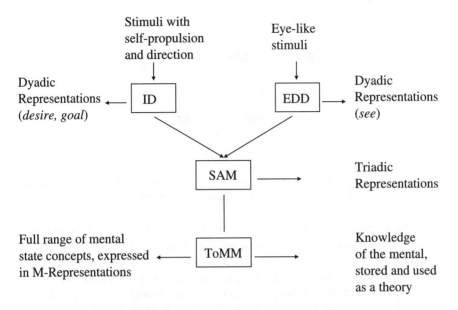

Figure 1.   *The mindreading system (reproduced, with kind permission of MIT Press, from Baron-Cohen 1995: 32)*

The EDD (eye direction detector) has three basic functions: "it detects the presence of eyes or eye like stimuli; it computes whether eyes are directed towards it or toward something else, and it infers from its own case that if another organism's eyes are directed at something then the organism sees that thing" (Baron-Cohen 1995: 38–9). This last function is crucial to a more advanced interactional understanding since it allows the child to attribute another perceptual state such as 'X sees me'. ID is based on volitional possibilities of desire and goal; EDD "interprets stimuli in relation to what the agent sees" (Baron-Cohen 1995: 39).

This is a fairly limited function on its own, but combined with SAM, 'the shared attention mechanism', things become much more interesting. The function of SAM is to build on the essential dyadic relations of ID and EDD (for example agent wants food or agent sees me) and creates more complex and interactive triadic relationships, or as Baron Cohen calls them 'triadic representations'. This is most easily explained using a simple diagram from Baron-Cohen (Fig. 2).

What can be seen here is that an agent may perceive an object and then receive input which indicates that another person is looking at the same object

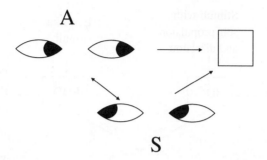

Figure 2.   *A pictorial representation of a triadic representation (reproduced, with kind
permission of MIT Press, from Baron-Cohen 1995: 45)*

(perhaps by noting the other person's eye direction); here then the agent may
build a representation of [P sees (I see the object)]. This is an example of
developing the ability to compute shared attention. This is only possible where
one compares an agent's perceptual state with one's own perceptual state.

The final and most complex component of the model is what is called the
theory of the mind mechanism (ToMM). The name is taken from Leslie's (1994)
model, and is different in so far as Baron-Cohen has introduced ID, EDD, and
SAM as developmental inputs to ToMM. ToMM is a system which represents
mental states operating over propositions, ToMM constructs representations of
propositional attitudes, referred to by Leslie (1994) as M-representations:

> [John believes- 'Liverpool are a good football team']
> [Tom thinks- 'Bill likes him']

The significance of ToMM for Baron-Cohen's model is that it is here that false
representations may take place. Imagine Mary sees a marble being placed in a
basket. She is then asked to leave the room. At this point the marble is removed
from the basket and placed in a cup. When Mary re-enters the room normal
subjects are able to compute Mary's belief regarding the location of the marble,
a belief which would now be false.

> [Mary thinks- 'the marble is in the basket']

If we treat this formal structure as an M-representation, then it is possible for the
whole representation to be true, when the proposition 'the marble is in the
basket' is false. This is a classic case of the problems of intensionality, or more
simply what is known as substitutability failure. If I believe that I have spoken
to Fred Watson, I might not also know that Fred Watson is my second cousin.

So while A would be true B would be false, even though both descriptions refer to the same person.

A.   John believes that he spoke to Fred Watson
B.   John believes that he spoke to his second cousin

The significance of this becomes apparent when we look at people who are unable to represent false belief, as for example found in autism. Given the information that Fred Watson is the same person as John's second cousin, but that John does not know this, speakers incapable of representing false belief would incorrectly impute B (see above) to John in such a context of belief. Equally, in the case of the marble example, a person incapable of representing a false belief might give the wrong response to a question such as 'Where will Mary look for the marble?', by saying that she will look in the cup (for examples of false belief in autism see Baron Cohen 1989; 1995; Gopnick and Wellman 1992; Happé 1994).

Baron-Cohen offers his model of mindreading within a modular framework of the mind (Fodor 1983;1987) and in this respect the mechanisms he outlines may be seen as operating independently, but interactively. In such a context, as Baron-Cohen observes, it would be possible for damage to occur in one system or another, with disability being reflected in relation to the specific system which was damaged. He follows this argument through at each level for ID, EDD, SAM and ToMM and describes how they function within autism. His findings suggest that while ID and EDD are intact and operational within autism, SAM reveals a significant impairment, and that since SAM is an essential input to ToMM, that autistic children will show a significant deficit here.

Such a claim has been clearly shown in the literature (for a review see Baron-Cohen 1995: ch.4) and it is now classic knowledge that autistic children have problems with false beliefs of the kind noted above, and therefore that SAM and ToMM may be severely impaired.

4.   Pragmatic Impairments, Beliefs, and A Theory of the Mind

Now how might all of this relate to our example of Child A above, or the more general claim that such children have difficulty constructing shared topics and maintaining reference across a range of turns. The first thing to note is that in order to negotiate talk around an object/topic one must focus joint attention on the object/topic. In this sense SAM would seem to be central. However, even if one were successful in gaining attention and directing joint focus on a topic or object, unless one also takes account of what the hearer knows or believes about that object relative to what one knows or believes about that object, i.e. unless one is able to represent different mental states (have a ToMM), then interactional progress will be limited.

But how does this actually work, and in what sense can it explain topic negotiation and reference? In order to move things forward here it would be useful to have a working model of how we represent objects/topics, and how we represent other's representations of objects/topics. Ballim and Wilks's (1992) model of artificial believers seems particularly appropriate here. Not only does their model of belief provide a way of thinking about representation, but because this model is, in one sense, an exercise in engineering (i.e. it is designed to run on a computer system) it can be shown to actually work — at one level of design.

The model developed by Ballim and Wilks (see also Wilks and Bein 1981) is relatively complex in its formal construction. However, the way in which the process operates may be straightforwardly explained by drawing on the following constructed dialogue (Ballim and Wilks 1992: 32–7).

USER: Frank is coming tomorrow I think
SYSTEM: Perhaps I should leave(*)
USER: Why?
SYSTEM: Coming from you that's a warning
USER: Does Frank dislike you?
SYSTEM: I don't know(**), but you think he does and that is what is
         important now

In this dialogue the system is said to run beliefs at points (*) and (**) within different 'belief environments'. These environments may represent John's beliefs about topics, as in (1), or John's beliefs about Bill's beliefs (about the same or other topics) as in (2):

(1)
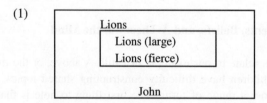

(2)

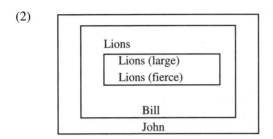

In (1) we have a representation of what John believes about 'lions' as a topic (topics are represented to the left of the top line of a beliefs environment: an enclosed area). In (2) we have a representation of what John believes about Bill's beliefs about 'lions'; in this case the beliefs are the same as those held by John.

Now in the case of the dialogue presented by Ballim and Wilks, they argue that the system is running beliefs within different environments at points (*) and (**). At point (*) it is an environment of the nested type as in (3). This nested set of beliefs is what the system believes the user believes Frank believes about the system. If in the inner box there is a representation 'Frank dislikes the system', this would account for the reaction at (*).

(3)

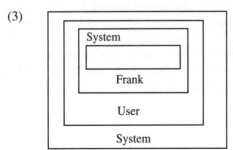

However, at point (**) the system runs beliefs in a different belief environment, reflecting this time only the system's own beliefs about Frank's beliefs about the system, as in (4).

(4)

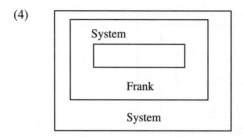

In this case the inner environment does not contain the representation 'Frank dislikes the system'. The system's own beliefs about what Frank believes about the system do not contain this information (hence the response 'I don't know').

As noted above there are a range of complexities and unresolved issues here, but for the moment accepting this way of representing beliefs about topics, and beliefs about others' beliefs about topics as a useful heuristic, we may make use of this approach, along with SAM and ToMM, to reflect on the potential problems displayed by Child A in reference and topic manipulation.

Before doing this directly, let us apply Ballim and Wilks's beliefs approach to the example of the 'marble' given above. In this example Mary re-enters a room but does not know that a marble previously located in a basket, has been moved from the basket into a cup. Our subject, let us call him X, remained in the room and does know the marble has been moved from the basket to the cup. If we ask the subject 'where will Mary look for the marble' the correct answer would be 'in the basket', because that is where she believes it to be. In Ballim and Wilks terms this may be represented as (5).

(5)

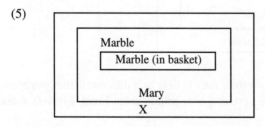

But what would an incorrect response such as 'Mary will look in the cup' look like in terms of belief environments? What reason would X have for generating such a belief environment on behalf of Mary? The classic response is that X does not generate any belief for Mary. Because of a defect in his theory of the mind he does not take account of Mary's beliefs but runs simply his own beliefs.

(6)

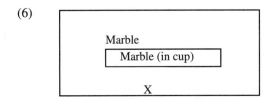

Put in this way the diagram would account for X's failure to give a correct response. But if this were true, while it would account for X's failure to take account of what Mary believes, it does not show how X takes account of Mary at all. Remember if the question is 'Where will *Mary* look for the marble?', the only way to explain the incorrect answer is to not only argue that X does not take account of Mary's beliefs, but also that either X treats the referential designate of 'Mary' as X himself, or that X has not taken account of 'Mary' as a referential term at all (and both may be to some extent related). This is indeed odd. But the Ballim and Wilks model offers us another way to account for the process, one in which the problem is that X runs Mary's beliefs as his own. In the Ballim and Wilks model when there is a clash of beliefs, this may be represented within the system's modelling of environments and then either resolved through corrective output, or maintained relative to different contexts (as in intensional cases). For example, if we combine (5) and (6), as in (7) we have a clash of beliefs. What X believes about the location of the marble differs from what Mary believes about the location of the marble. X, functioning as a normal subject, is able to represent this fact, and adjust representations in response to questions such as 'where will Mary look for the marble' (see (5)). Ballim and Wilks refer to the movement of environments from outer nesting to inner nesting as 'belief ascription'. So in (7) if X attempts to move what Mary believes about the location of the marble into the environment of beliefs that X has about the location of the marble then there will be a clash reflecting the divergence of beliefs based on their different experiences. If we look at Mary's case, however, she not only believes that the marble is in the basket, but believes X believes this:

(7)

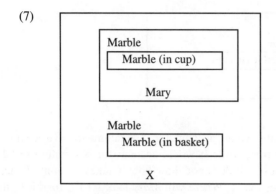

For Mary ascription is straightforward. If asked where X would look for the marble, the answer from Mary's point of view is the same place as her.

Now as Baron-Cohen has suggested, within a modular system damage may occur at various places. If we assume that internal to a system such as ToMM is a belief representation programme such as that suggested by Ballim and Wilks, then it seems possible that damage might occur here, at a sub modular level if you like. Let us further imagine that damage may occur to the ascription process such that either (a) one cannot represent others' beliefs (the failure of the theory of the mind: which would also have to account for where and how 'Mary' is represented, even if no beliefs about her beliefs were involved); or (b) one can represent others' beliefs but that ascription has in some sense failed to work correctly; working outwards, perhaps, instead of inwards in nested environments, and that the default of the system is to accept its own beliefs as being the same as that of another. Interestingly the default starting point of the Ballim and Wilks model is to assume that one's beliefs are the same as others' unless one has information to the contrary. If, however, due to some level of modular ascription damage one deleted or wrote one's own beliefs over another's then one's behaviour would look like that of someone who did not have a theory of the mind, instead of potentially someone who does have a theory of the mind but who cannot operationalise it due to damage at one level or other of the belief representation process. In this case X could represent what Mary believes about the marble, but in the process of constructing her beliefs overwrite them with his own. In other words X has a theory of the mind process, other minds exist, but because of failure at the level of ascription they are represented as X's own. This is a speculative claim, but none the less plausible (or radical) for that. But it is also perhaps more than this. The advantage of this sub modular explanation is that it might account for the proportion of autistic children who succeed at first order false belief tasks (running beliefs of Mary *re* the marble: Baron-Cohen, Leslie and Frith 1988; Baron-Cohen 1995: 72), but who fail when the task is presented at a second order level of nested beliefs (Baron-Cohen 1989) i.e. having to run X's beliefs about Mary's beliefs about the location of the marble ('where do you believe X believes Mary will look for the marble?'). This greater level of embedding of beliefs and the control required to run two belief environments relative to each other and to one's own, clearly makes the task more complex. The increased complexity should not, however, lead us to assume that such children have now lost their theory of the mind previously available on a first order task. It seems more plausible that in an already weakened system of ToMM, the ascription process of beliefs may be limited to first order possibilities. Those children who fail in the first order task may simply show even greater limits on the operation of ascription, but not necessarily of the ToMM itself. The importance of the example for the purposes of this chapter is to show the heuristic advantages of the Ballim and Wilks model of beliefs representation: and this would seem to have relevance whether one adopts the traditional theory of the mind explanation of the marble example, or the more radical sub modular alternative suggested above.

Now how does this beliefs and theory of the mind approach allow us to offer an explanation for Child A's behaviour. Well, let us imagine that the child has a series of beliefs about the topic Dragon's eyes (we never discovered what this was, so these are simply plausible topic elements), for example: Dragon's Eyes is a TV programme; in it some space traveller must bring back a certain number of Phetons, each of which represent the energy of Pellamar and must be returned to save the earth, but there are only so many left; today one of the Phetons exploded; cf. (8).

Since the Child has been asked in the first turn what was going on in the classroom he accesses his beliefs about that domain and the central role of the Dragon's Eyes. Now, what he should also access here in normal topic construction is some representation of the beliefs of the therapist regarding the topic of the Dragon's eyes. A normal representation would be something like (9).

(8)

(9)

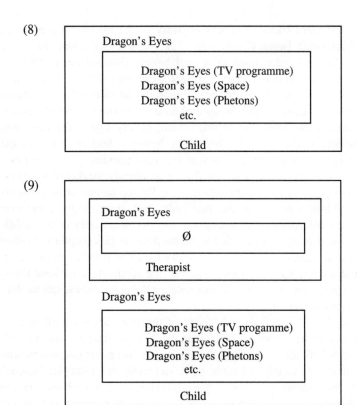

Here there are no beliefs about Dragon's Eyes within the environment for the therapist. And normal ascription processes (nesting the therapist's beliefs within the Child's beliefs) will highlight this difference. In this case accessibility issues of the kind described by Ariel (1990) would go into action. That is the speaker would need to introduce the topic by a range of low accessibility routes, which simply means that definite noun phrase forms should be employed with further description until the listener has all the requisite objects in mind to allow the use of high accessibility markers such as pronominal forms like *he, she, they* and *it*. The Child does employ a definite noun phrase low accessibility marker initially at (2.), but does not follow through on further detail to allow the therapist to construct beliefs about objects relevant to Dragon's eyes similar to those held by the Child. This might be explained in the same way as the false belief case, by either assuming (a) that Child A does not have a theory of the mind, and therefore does not construct a beliefs environment for the therapist, or (b) that the Child ascribes beliefs to the therapist regarding *Dragon's eyes* which are the same as his own, beliefs cf. (10). Possibility (a), however, suffers from the fact that in many other places during the session the child does take account (at some level) of what the therapist knows.

Possibility (b) could account for this difference however, and further account for the fact that the child carries on extending the topic in inappropriate circumstances, and why he makes use of high accessibility markers at an inappropriate time.

(10)

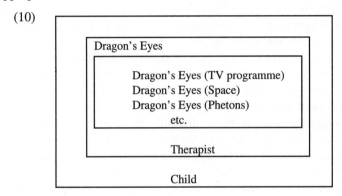

Within such an account the Child may be shown to have an intact understanding of general reference principles, i.e. he does follow low accessibility markers with high accessibility markers as one would predict. The problem is that accessibility here is internal to the child's beliefs system rather than any shared belief system. But even here we could argue that the Child would have the ability to understand the need for shared attention as in SAM, and even how this should be fed into ToMM, the problem is that the representations fed in by the Child turn out to be his own, and therefore not that of the other. So where is the problem? Indicators are that SAM is intact. If so this suggests that one is taking account of another's viewpoint. The problem seems to be, therefore, that in representing another's beliefs the child ends up representing his own. But why would this be the case? One obvious and perhaps simple response is that processing loads may affect the way in which the embedding of belief ascription proceeds (as noted in second order processing above). As the processing load increases it becomes harder to maintain the monitoring of others' beliefs. This would explain why such children can talk with others more easily about objects present and in view as opposed to those that have to be transposed from memory and compared with those another speaker/hearer may or may not have in mind. This might also account for those autistic children who prove successful in simple or first order false belief tests but who have more difficulty with second order belief tests (for example, Kevin thinks that Bills thinks the marble is in the basket.)

But how does this all relate to pragmatic impairment? Accessibility is a pragmatic concept in so far as the choice of topic and referential markers are relevant to what has been or can be accessed at a point in time. This is a joint activity in most cases and, therefore, monitoring of joint access in relation to linguistic selection is a pragmatic issue. In the case of the semantic-pragmatic impaired child the monitoring has been disrupted to such an extent that accessibility selection is operating on a single rather than joint track, and as a result the output is pragmatically inappropriate.

One of the difficulties with the type of explanation offered above is that it seems to be cognitive, or social cognitive at least, and this raises questions about whether the problem is pragmatic at all — at least if one sees pragmatics within a narrow linguistic framework. This problem is noted by Perkins (this volume), and he has suggested that pragmatic disability may operate at a number of different levels, i.e. Primary Pragmatic Disability; Secondary Pragmatic Disability; and Complex Pragmatic Disability. The first suggests intact linguistics with communicative performance impaired through a failure, or problem, within central processing systems such as inference; use of world knowledge; memory and so on. The second indicates communicative impairment not due to non-linguistic cognitive impairment, here reflecting difficulties in syntax/morphology; word finding difficulties (lexis); problems of phonology or prosody. And the third reflects that the first two (perhaps not surprisingly) are not mutually exclusive and may be jointly revealed in some cases.

This is an interesting way of considering the issues, but as we noted at the outset we view pragmatics as being located at the interface of linguistic and cognitive issues. The neat separation of types of disability would, we believe, be difficult to maintain. For example, some words, claimed to be presuppositional (such as *regret* and *manage*), would seem to have inferential and reasoning issues built into them (see Levinson 1983; see also Mey 1993 who argues that many more linguistic forms carry inherent social meaning); equally, difficulties of lexical location could be memory constrained, or reflect only lexical problems; or where does the social knowledge available at a sociolinguistic level reside; this is often quantitatively marked and matched to social facts, yet at the same time systematically constrained by the language itself (see Labov 1995). Modularity is useful in so far as it suggests ways of understanding different operating systems. In communication, normal or disordered, it seems logical that one system may be disfunctioning while others are not; indeed this is, in part, what we have argued above. We are not convinced, however, of the need to separate types of disorder in any strict way at this stage of our understanding, although we are all in favour of drawing attention to the interaction of complex sets of knowledge revealed in everyday communication.

5. Beliefs about Therapy

We have argued above that Child A may have a problem located in the use of belief ascription, within the general process of what Baron-Cohen calls mind-reading. Given certain types of online load or overload, the child treats others' beliefs about the world as the same as his own. Problems of topic negotiation obviously emerge, and other referential deficits may simply fall out as a consequence of ascription difficulties. We believe this argument is plausible, as far as it goes, and offers some account of what may be happening in the case of Child A and others like him. But assuming what we have said is on the right track, what kind of possible therapy would one attempt with such a child, or with the class of children (perhaps including autism) of which he is a representative. In this section we offer some basic thoughts on this question.

Therapists' own beliefs about therapy are challenged when intervention shifts from the more traditional areas of therapy such as phonology, syntax and semantics. As already discussed, the difficulties exhibited by children described as having a 'pragmatic impairment' (Craig 1995) fall within the domain of socio-cognition. This is hardly surprising when we consider what the term pragmatics actually encompasses: "not only linguistics, cognitive science, cultural anthropology and philosophy, logic, semantic action theory but also sociology, interpersonal dynamics and social convention and rhetoric contribute to its domain" (Green 1989).

As therapists we need to be fully aware of the scope of the term pragmatics and the areas it encompasses. Baron-Cohen (1988) suggests that "almost all pragmatic skills require a theory of mind (which is itself a metarepresentational capacity)". Therefore, therapy directed towards pragmatic impairment must also be directed at socio-cognitive abilities. In this sense, and taking account of our arguments in this chapter, one could suggest a therapy model which initially targets perspective taking ability in its broadest sense. From here one could then move towards more finely graded tasks requiring higher order representations of beliefs.

Despite the abstract nature of some of our descriptions, there are examples of relevant approaches within the literature. Dawson and Fernald (1987) outline a variety of tasks which could form the basis of an approach aimed at improving a child's ability to ascribe beliefs to another person. They divide perspective taking into three areas: perceptual role taking, conceptual role taking and affective role taking. Under the heading 'perceptual role taking' one such task, the 'upside down' task, is outlined. This consists of a card with a black and white drawing of a boy standing up. This card is then placed crosswise between the child and the adult. The child is asked to show the boy to the adult so that the adult could see him standing on his head. Under the heading 'conceptual role taking' the child might be asked to relate a selection of 'gifts' i.e. a necklace, a tie, a doll to the appropriate recipient such as mother, father, sister (Flavelle *et al.* 1975, Zahn-Waxler *et al.*, 1977 in Dawson and Fernald 1987). Under 'affective role taking' the child might be asked to look at four faces: happy, sad, afraid, angry. Once the child can recognise and name the emotions the child could be shown a series of pictures of another child with a blank face in various situations which would typically elicit one of the above emotional responses, for example, being alone in the dark etc. A short story could accompany the presentation of each picture (Borke 1971, in Dawson and Fernald 1987).

These and many similar activities will help the child to begin to appreciate in a general sense another's perspective. At a more advanced level stories could be introduced which might be 'loaded' with anaphoric pronouns to test the child's comprehension and ability to locate a coreferential in connected speech. Retelling of stories could also be used to encourage correct use of the referential aspects of communication discussed earlier. Higher level tasks involving irony and metaphor could also be introduced with older children to target higher order beliefs. Once we have a clear idea of the abilities underlying pragmatic competence then as therapists we can begin to devise therapy tasks which will help improve a child's pragmatic ability. With children described as having 'pragmatic impairment' we have no choice in shifting our interventions away from traditional areas, since as Aarons and Gittens (1992) suggest, these children's deficits: 'are not confined to language alone'.

These comments are, of course, merely suggestive, but should, we hope, indicate, if our modelling of Child A's problem is correct, one avenue of therapy which might be useful in moving forward this child's communicative ability from pragmatically impaired to pragmatically normal.

6.   Conclusions and Summary

We have argued in this chapter that if we wish to understand the therapeutic implications of pragmatic impairment we need first to articulate what we believe such impairments to be; only then are we in a position to consider what forms of relevant therapy, if any, are appropriate. In looking at the problem displayed by Child A we took into account what may, at first, seem to be divergent theoretical models of how we process our beliefs of others relative to our own beliefs. Baron-Cohen's (1995) view of mindreading is evolutionary and developmental, while Ballim and Wilks' (1992) description of belief ascription is engineered for production as programmed output. Nevertheless, and particularly at the level of ToMM, they are useful guides to understanding not only how beliefs about the beliefs of others may operate, but also what happens when the process goes wrong. By combining these approaches we have offered a theoretical account of the potential problems faced by Child A. In doing so we have raised many questions which we are far from answering; for example, two major issues of interest would be how do deficits in ascription relate to modularity? And can the kind of deficit we have described be modelled on a computer, such that it can be made to simulate the behaviour of Child A? The first question raises a host of abstract issues, while the second raises interesting possibilities for the future. Whatever the case, the answers to the problems of children like Child A are not going to be simple, and we should be prepared to look in several directions at once in the search for solutions, for such, in our view, is the nature of pragmatics.

References

Aarons, N. and Gittens, T. 1992. *The Handbook of Autism: A Guide for Parents and Professionals*. London:Routledge.

Ariel, M. 1990. *Accessibility*. London: Routledge.

Bach, K. 1994. "Conversational implicature". *Mind and Language* 9(2): 125–161.

Ballim, A. and Wilks, Y. 1992. *Artifical Believers*. Hove: LEA.

Baren-Cohen, S. 1988. "Social and pragmatic deficits in autism: cognitive or affective?". *Journal of Autism and Developmental Disorders* 18: 379–402.

Baron-Cohen, S. 1995. *Mindblindness: An Essay on Autism and Theory of Mind*. London and Cambridge Mass: MIT Press.

Baron-Cohen, S. 1989. "The autistic child's theory of the mind: A case of specific developmental delay". *Journal of Child Psychology and Child Psychiatry* 30: 285–298.

Bilgrami, A. 1996. *Belief and Meaning*. Oxford: Blackwell.

Clark, H. H. and Wilkes-Gibbs, D. 1986. "Referring as a collaborative process". *Cognition* 22: 1–39.

Craig, H. K. 1995. "Pragmatic impairments". In *The Handbook of Child Language*, P. Fletcher and B. MacWhinney (eds), 623–640. Oxford: Blackwell.

Danes, F. 1974. *Papers on Functional Sentence Perspective*. The Hague: Mouton.

Dawson, G. and Fernald, M. 1987. "Perspective taking ability and its relationship to the social behaviour of autistic children". *Journal of Autism and Developmental Disorders* 17(4): 487–497.

Fodor, J. A. 1983. *The Modularity of the Mind*. Cambridge MA: MIT Press.

Fodor, J. A. 1987. *Psychosemantics*. Cambridge, MA: MIT Press.

Green, G. M. 1989. *Pragmatics and Natural Language Understanding*. Hillsdale, NJ: L. Erlbaum.

Gopnick, A. and Wellman, H. 1992. "Why the child's theory of the mind really is a theory". *Mind and Language* 7: 145–171.

Happé, F. 1994. "Communicative Competence and theory of the mind in autisim. A test of relevance theory". *Cognition* 48: 101–119.

Heider, F. and Simmel, M. 1944. "An experimental study of apparent behaviour". *American Journal of Psychology* 57: 243–259.

Johnson-Laird, P. 1983. *Mental Models*. Cambridge: Cambridge University Press.

Kintsch, W, and Van Dijk, T. 1978. "Toward a model of text comprehension and production". *Psychological Review* 85: 363–394.

Labov, W. 1995. *Principles of Linguistic Change* . Oxford: Blackwell.

Leonard, L. 1986. "Conversational replies of children with specific language impairment." *Journal of Speech and Hearing Research* 29: 114–119.

Leonard, L., Camarata, S., Rowan, L., and Chapman, K. 1982. "The communicative functions of lexical usage by language impaired children". *Applied Psycholinguistics* 3: 109–25.

Leslie, A. 1987. "Pretense and representation. The orgins of 'theory of the mind'". *Psychological Review* 94: 412–16.

Leslie, A. 1994. "ToMM, ToBY, and Agency: Domain architecture and domain specificity". In *Mapping the Mind: Domain Specificity in Cognition and Culture*, L. Hurchfield and S. Felman (eds). Cambridge: Cambridge University Press.

Leslie, A., and Frith, U. 1988. "Autistic children's understanding of seeing, knowing, and believing". *British Journal of Developmental Psychology* 6: 315–334.

Levinson, S. C. 1983. *Pragmatics*. Cambridge: Cambridge University Press.

MacWhinney, B. 1991. "Connectionism as a framework for language acquisition theory". In *Research on Child Language Disorders: A Decade of Progress*, J. Miller (ed.). Austin, Texas: Pro Ed.

McAnulty, L. 1996. *Semantic/Pragmatic Disorders*. Unpublished MPhil thesis, University of Ulster.

McTear, M. F. and Conti-Ramsden, G. 1992. *Pragmatic Disability in Children*. London: Whurr.

Mey, J. L. 1993. *Pragmatics: An Introduction*. Oxford: Blackwell.

Minsky, M. 1975. "A framework for representing knowledge". In *Psychology of Computer Vision*, P. H. Winston (ed.). New York: McCraw Hill.

Rapin, I. and Allen, D. A. 1983. "Developmental language disorders: Nosologic considerations". In *Neuropsychology of Language, Reading, and Spelling*, U. Kirk (ed.), 155–184. New York: Academic Press.

Recanati, F. 1993. *Direct Reference: from Language to Thought*. Oxford: Blackwell.

Sacks, H. and Schegloff, E. 1979. "Two preferences in the organisation of reference to persons in conversation and their interaction". In *Everyday Language Studies in Ethnomethodology*, Psathas, G. (ed.). Hillsdale, N. J.: Erlbaum.

Sacks, H., Schegloff, E. and Jefferson, G. 1975. "A simplest systematics for the organsiation of turn taking in conversation." In *Studies in the Organisation of Conversational Interaction*, J. Schenkein (ed.). New York: Academic Press.

Schank, R. C. and Abelson, R. P. 1977. *Scripts, Plans, Goals and Understanding*. Hillsdale NJ: LEA.

Schober, M. F. and Clark, H. 1989. "Understanding by addressees and overhearers." *Cognitive Psychology* 21: 211–32.

Searle, J. 1983. *Intentionality*. Oxford: Oxford University Press.

Smith, B. R. and Leinonen, E. 1992. *Clinical Pragmatics: Unravelling the Complexities of Communicative Failure*. London: Chapman and Hall.

Sperber, D. and Wilson, D. 1996. *Relevance*. 2nd edition. Oxford: Blackwell.

Stubbs, M. W. 1986. *Educational Linguistics*. Oxford:Blackwell.

Van Kleeck, A., and Frankel, T. 1981. "Discourse devices used by language disordered children: a preliminary investigation". *Journal of Speech and Hearing Disorders* 46: 250–257.

Wilks, Y. and Bein, J. 1981. *Beliefs, Points of View and Multiple Environments*. Cognitive Studies Centre: University of Essex.

Wilson, J. 1989. *On The Boundaries of Conversation*. Oxford: Pergamon.

Maximising Communication Effectiveness

Alison Ferguson

University of Newcastle, New South Wales

1. Introduction

Sociolinguistic perspectives on communication disorder allow us to recognise that effective communication requires a *multilayered* and *dynamic* process of negotiation of meaning between *both* partners in the exchange. This chapter presents an overview of the theoretical and empirical research which looks at the notion of 'communication strategies' from conversation and discourse analytic perspectives. Current views as to what constitutes strategic communication are challenged, and an alternative framework is proposed, based on applications of sociolinguistics within the field of second language acquisition. Implications of this framework are discussed in relation to both assessment and treatment.[1]

In the following discussion, the perspectives on language from both psycholinguistics and sociolinguistics are contrasted in order to highlight their complementary contributions to an understanding of disordered communication. Each of these perspectives is built on a fundamentally different notion of the context of communication. Context can be defined as comprising the "...social and psychological world in which the language user operates at any given time" (Ochs and Schieffelin 1979: 1). This broad definition encapsulates the way psycholinguistic and sociolinguistic perspectives differ in their view of language and context. The key distinctions can be presented as:

Psycholinguistic	*Sociolinguistic*
Individual	Joint
Code	Multilayered
Static	Dynamic

From a psycholinguistic perspective, language is that psychological product (whether uttered or as some form of cognitive representation of a language rule system) of the individual, which is common to all individuals (universally or intra-culturally). From this perspective then, language is considered within the context of the psychological world to comprise the abstract representation of the language system, or 'code' (as Sperber and Wilson 1986, 1995, describe this aspect of language). Other psychological (e.g. emotion) and social (e.g. activity) aspects of context are, in a sense, described 'negatively', in that only those manifestations of language which show no variation are seen as part of the language system. Thus, from a psycholinguistic perspective, control is sought over contextual variation, in order to achieve a static description and explanation of language.

From a sociolinguistic perspective, the internal psychological language of the individual is seen as both arising from the external socio-cultural world, and as having effects upon it. Within the field of sociolinguistics, the perspective of Pragmatics has attempted to describe and explain the relationship between aspects of context and language use (Leech 1983), while the perspective of Discourse Analysis has focussed upon the description and explanation of the ways in which language is used to express contextual meanings (Stubbs 1983). Within the field of Discourse Analysis, the semantic perspective of Systemic Functional Linguistics argues for the inseparability of meanings within a language text and the multilayered aspects of the context in which the language text arises (Halliday 1985). The dynamic aspects of language use are well described through the approach of Conversation Analysis, which is derived from the sociological approach of ethnography (Benson and Hughes 1983).

In order to examine communication effectiveness, this chapter presents a view of language as the joint product of individuals continuously influenced by their socio-cultural environment. The psychological world is seen as influenced by the social world, and contextual variation is explored, in order to achieve a description and explanation of the dynamic nature of language in use. Figure 1 presents a more detailed description of the gradations between the psycho-linguistic and sociolinguistic perspectives on language, with regard to the way they view aspects of context.

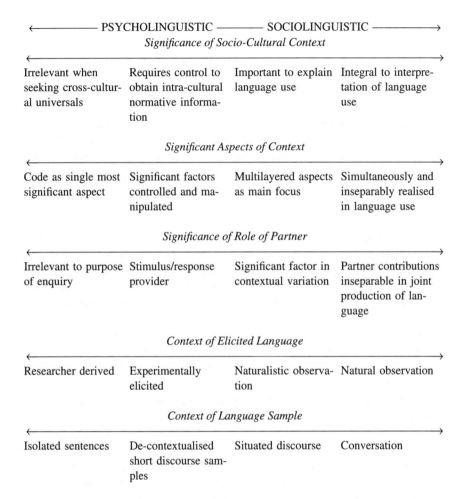

Figure 1. *Psycholinguistic and Sociolinguistic Perspectives on Language Context*

Turning now to consider how we might go about maximising communication effectiveness, we need to consider firstly what we mean by 'communication' and what we mean by 'effectiveness'. We also need to examine critically what we consider to be 'maximising' such effectiveness, i.e. what exactly are we trying to achieve?

2.   Effective Communication

What do we mean when we describe communication as effective? From traditional psycholinguistic perspectives, communication is seen as concerned primarily with the message itself — as encoded and decoded information. Whether the message is effective depends on whether the encoding or decoding processes are accurate, i.e. does the decoded message match the encoded message? From sociolinguistic perspectives (including those described as 'pragmatic'), such a message-bound view is seen as too narrowly circumscribed in failing to recognise that communication is multilayered and dynamic in nature.

2.1 Multilayered

The problem faced when considering the many aspects of context is not so much in recognising that there are relationships between aspects of language and aspects of context, but rather in identifying *which* aspects of socio-cultural context are salient for the conduct of conversation (Berger and Bradac 1982; Werth 1984). There is general agreement amongst sociolinguistic views of language that the salient aspects of context involve the activity being carried out at the time, the relationship between the interactants, and the role language is playing in organising or actualising the meanings being exchanged. Table 1 presents a comparison of the contextual aspects highlighted in sociolinguistic perspectives on language.

Many linguistic perspectives have recognised the multilayered nature of communication, and the description of the three main 'metafunctions' of language provided by the semantic perspective of Systemic Functional Linguistics (Halliday 1985; Halliday and Hasan 1985) encapsulates the general consensus that it is important to recognise that any act of communication is simultaneously *about something* (experiential metafunction — the 'field' aspect of context), *between interactants* (interpersonal metafunction — the 'tenor' aspect of context), and *uses language* (textual metafunction — the 'mode' aspect of context). This deceptively simple description of the multilayered nature of language use in context bears closer examination, for this description deals with two major issues which present theoretical and practical difficulties from pragmatic perspectives. These issues are the simultaneous functions of language use, and the relationship of text to context, for without a way of dealing with these two issues, our understanding of communication remains uni-dimensional.

Table 1.   *Aspects of Context*

What is going on	Who are taking part	Role of language	As discussed by
Field	Tenor	Mode	Halliday (1978) Halliday & Hasan (1985)
Global	Interaction	Utterance	Bremer *et al.* (1987)
Situation, Topic	Role	Prior message	Berger & Bradac (1982)
Setting, Purpose, Message content	Participants	Key, Channel	Coulthard (1985)

Field is described by Halliday and Hasan (1985: 45–46) as including "the kind of activity as recognised in the culture within which language is playing some part". The field of discourse is seen as influencing what is talked about and for what purposes. The aspect of communication effectiveness most affected by the field of discourse is that of the accuracy/adequacy of the content of the messages exchanged. *Tenor* is described by Halliday and Hasan (ibid.) as "the interacting roles that are involved in the creation of texts", and this aspect of context is seen as reflecting the nature of the interpersonal relationships involved in the exchange, e.g. relative power, status, control, solidarity, divergence. The aspect of communication effectiveness most affected by the tenor of discourse is that of the interpersonal harmony established and being maintained between the participants in the exchange. *Mode* is described by Halliday and Hasan (ibid.) as the "particular functions that are assigned to language" in the situation, and so this aspect of context involves the way the form of the utterances produced (including the organisation of utterances and channels) is used to realise meanings in the situation. The aspect of communication effectiveness most affected is the coherence of the exchange.

In the Systemic Functional Linguistic approach different aspects of context are related to different functions of language, and it can be argued that this approach provides a richer description of the communication than available from other sociolinguistic approaches involving description of 'speech acts'. With regard to the functions of language, speech pathologists will be very familiar with functional views of communication which arise from pragmatic perspectives such as speech act theory (Austin 1975; Grice 1975; Searle 1969). The most widely used clinical application of these views has been to describe instances of language use with regard to what speech act is being performed (e.g. Wilcox and Davis 1977; Skinner, Wirz, Thompson and Davidson 1984; Wirz, Skinner and Dean 1990). In the practical application of this approach, many speech pathologists will have experienced the frustration and irritation with having to choose which speech act is being performed — e.g. Can you open the door? — a question or a demand? This practical problem is a direct reflection of the theoretical dilemma here — there are potentially an infinite number of speech acts (as many as there are verbs in the language, some are heard to say!), and more importantly with regard to the issue at hand, any one utterance may perform many functions simultaneously, i.e. for the preceding example, it is *both* a question and a demand. Halliday's description of the three metafunctions are 'meta' because they are the main functions of every utterance on every occasion. For the preceding example, the utterance is a request for services (experiential function), reflecting a particular (demanding) power relationship between the participants (interpersonal function), and mediated through an interrogative (question) form in the text (textual function). With this recognition of the simultaneous realisation of multiple layers of meaning, it becomes possible to recognise the importance of considering all layers as part of the communication. The relationship of aspects of context and each metafunction is summarised thus:

Context	Metafunction
Field	Experiential/Ideational
Tenor	Interpersonal
Mode	Textual

The second issue upon which the Systemic Functional Linguistic perspective sheds some further light is the relationship of text to context. Sociolinguistic perspectives often seem to fall in one of two camps — those that focus solely on discourse as text (e.g. Van Dijk 1980) and those pragmatic approaches that focus on interpersonal and sociological aspects (e.g. Brown and Levinson's 1987 treatment of politeness). The Systemic Functional Linguistic perspective proposes that particular aspects of context are realised through particular aspects of text — or equally, particular aspects of text reflect particular aspects of context. In the preceding example, the textual realisation in the form of the interrogative reversal of Subject and Finite shows how the Mood system is used to reflect the Tenor of the relationship (Martin 1987). If the interpersonal relationship between participants were different, then choices made within the Mood system would reflect this, e.g. 'Might you possibly consider opening the door?'. When we consider communication in context then, we are also considering how the utterance makes use of the textual resources of the language and how this use reflects the broader social meanings of the context or situation. The relationship between the metafunctions and aspects of the lexico-grammar can be summarised as follows:

Metafunction	*Realised by Lexico-Grammar* *(examples)*
Experiential/Ideational	Transitivity
Interpersonal	Modality
Textual	Cohesion

In summary then, when we consider an individual's communication, we need to be aware of the way communication is at all times multilayered, and related to the context in which it occurred. If we are then to consider the effectiveness of that communication, we are interested no longer in the accuracy of the coded message transfer alone. We can consider the extent to which the utterance conveyed its experiential meaning — did it do what it set out to do? e.g. provide information, request goods or services. We can consider the extent to which the utterance contributed to the interpersonal exchange (positively or negatively). We can consider how effectively the resources of language were used to do both these things, as well as what channels of communication were used (spoken, gestural, written), and how coherently the utterance related to the preceding utterance(s). We can also consider how appropriate the use of language was for the larger social context with regard to each metafunction, e.g. type, amount and relevance of information (experiential); politeness, familiarity and power (interpersonal); lexical selection and density (textual). Example (1) illustrates some of the main points raised in this section.

(1)   *Aphasic/Normal Interaction*
       (25A/27NLF(neighbour) Conversation, Tape 123–125)
       A   Yes, and um, are you getting up to ... (UNINTELLIGIBLE)
            /koʊl, koʊl/ (LAUGHS)
       N   Up to, Newcastle?
       A   /wɛst koʊst, wɛst, wɛst koʊ/ I always have trouble with this
            one!
       N   Newcastle.
       A   /wɛ/ yes. /wɛndəl/ (LAUGHS). That's where I want to go!

In Example (1), a 60 year old aphasic man is talking with his 27 year old male neighbour. The field of discourse overall could be described as casual conversation on the topic of the neighbour's plans for a weekend trip. The tenor of the discourse can be described as involving same gender aquaintances with a significant age difference. The mode of discourse is spoken dialogue. At the moment of the example, the pair are involved in repairing some trouble in the conversation which has arisen from the aphasic individual's communication difficulties, and so at that moment the field of the discourse turns to look at the textual aspects of language itself, and the tenor shifts to involve a helping relationship. As is not uncommon in aphasic/normal dyads, the normal partner uses few politeness markers (e.g. through the modality system), but does use a questioning (rising) intonation on his first, but not second, instance of supplying the word for the aphasic partner. As has been suggested elsewhere (Ferguson 1992b) there may be a trade-off when repairing trouble, such that interpersonal aspects such as marking politeness may be exchanged for the textual demands of maintaining the cohesion and flow of the discourse through rapid and thereby discrete repair.

2.2 Dynamic

There is a tendency within both psycholinguistic and sociolinguistic approaches to view communication as 'product' rather than as 'process'. So, within some psycholinguistic approaches, it is the code itself which is the primary focus of investigation, e.g. Grodzinsky (1988). The recent developments in cognitive neuropsychological understandings of language, similarly focus their attention on the abstract structure of language, e.g. Byng and Black (1989), Coltheart (1987), Marshall (1995). However, within other psycholinguistic appproaches, it is the processing of language which is seen as the primary focus, e.g. connectionism (Harley 1993). These recent developments considering the inhibitory and facilitatory processes of language strike resonating chords with longstanding work in aphasiology by Schuell (Duffy 1994) and Porch (1994).

To give an example of these two different views, a product focus might highlight the alterations in semantic representation following aphasia, e.g. concrete words vs abstract. On the other hand, a process focus might highlight the facilitatory effects of cueing for word retrieval. This split in emphasis occurs also with sociolinguistic approaches, where discourse oriented approaches view the text as a unified product, and seek to understand its structure. However, sociolinguistic approaches drawing on the ethnomethodological tradition (Hammersley and Atkinson 1983) of Conversation Analysis focus primarily on the process of communication. A product focus looks at how different parts of a completed monologic text interrelate, e.g. analysis of cohesion. On the other hand, a process focus might look at how alternating speakers in a dialogue use repetition of each others' previous utterances in order to take the floor.

The methodology developed in Conversation Analysis (Atkinson and Heritage 1984; Boden and Zimmerman 1991) allows us to recognise that communication changes from moment-to-moment. For example, even within one speaker's turn, the topic may shift in response to some internal or external event and along with such a shift, occur adjustments in word choice and grammatical construction. From this view, rather than two speakers being engaged in sending and receiving some pre-set message, speakers can be observed to negotiate the meaning of a jointly produced exchange from turn to turn as the conversation unfolds.

An equally dynamic analysis is available from the perspective of Systemic Functional Linguistics, through what is termed, 'exchange analysis'. While early work within this perspective tended to be product oriented, e.g. cohesion analysis (Halliday and Hasan 1976), later work has applied key tenets of the perspective in a more process oriented approach, e.g. the analysis of casual conversation by Halliday and Plum (1985), and the development of exchange analysis (Berry 1981; Martin 1992). Exchange analysis from this perspective is proving to be productive for the analysis of communication problems following head injury (Togher, Code and Hand 1995). However, for the purposes of this chapter this form of semantic analysis does not offer a distinctive contribution to our understanding of the dynamic nature of conversation than is available from Conversation Analysis (CA), and so this latter — more 'pragmatic' perspective has been adopted.

When considering the effectiveness of communication from this dynamic framework then, we need to consider how the speakers manage this process of negotiation. Many researchers have looked at this, investigating turns or 'moves' in an exchange, e.g. Goodwin (1981) drawing from Duncan's (1975) work, Berry (1981) from Systemic Functional Linguistics, and the highly influential work of Sacks, Schegloff and Jefferson from the perspective of Conversation Analysis. Such sociolinguistic perspectives on turntaking are also compatible with psycho-linguistic frameworks as discussed in the work of Clark and Wilkes-Gibbs (1986). One area of particular interest to researchers in aphasia (and other communication disorders) is the conduct of repair (Schegloff, Jefferson and Sacks 1977) as the primary mechanism for this process of adjustment and negotiation between speakers (Lubinski, Duchan and Weitzner-Lin 1980; Milroy and Perkins 1992; Ferguson 1994; Perkins 1995).[2] Study of repair in conversation serves to show how speakers confirm, clarify, correct, and extend their own and others' messages. In analysing repair the movement of responsibility for trouble in conversation and its repair is mapped as it moves from speaker to speaker, e.g. repair 'trajectories' of same turn self-repair, next turn self-repair, next turn other-repair, other-initiated self-repair (prompts, cues), self-initiated other-repair (appeals for assistance).

Recognising the dynamic nature of communication means that we can turn even further away from the narrow question as to whether the message was accurate, and toward the broader issue of the processes by which mutual understanding is reached (Grimshaw 1980). Example (2), illustrates some of the main points regarding the need to consider the dynamic nature of communication.

(2)   *Aphasic/Normal Interaction*
       (1A(husband)/2NF(wife) Conversation, Tape 10–16)

   A   An a new ah club, a new one came. He's got a /smoʊk, smoʊ/, same me.
        He's ah, he's a /ʌnʌmə/. You know (UNINTELLIGIBLE) die. He died. /doʊn/ he, at that time died.
   N   They thought he was dead?
   A   No.
   N   Oh.
   A   He said it (UNINTELLIGIBLE), he was one. His, he (UNINTELLIGIBLE) died. And burned and things. He does it.
   N   Oh, he was, at cremation, worked at the cremation place did he?
   A   Yes

In Example (2), an aphasic man is discussing with his wife a recent visit to the Stroke Club, and his considerable word-finding difficulties have meant that his wife needs further clarification. The aphasic individual is undertaking frequent attempts at self-repair, and these repairs form the basis of the co-textual information upon which the wife appears to be basing her guesses as to the message. The wife initiates other repair, but her questioning intonation renders her repairs as potential prompts for the aphasic individual to self-repair if possible (i.e. other-initiated self-repair). In the event, however, the aphasic individual's subsequent responses 'switch' the trajectory back to 'other-initiated other-repair' by simply confirming or negating the accuracy of the other-repair.

2.3 *Responsibility*

The recognition of the dynamic nature of communication involves a shift from focussing on just one of the individuals in the exchange, to a focus on the jointly shared responsibility for communication of all participants in the exchange. When only one speaker's contribution is studied, then we tend to think of the effectiveness of communication as relating to that speaker's 'competence' or 'proficiency' (Lantolf and Frawley 1988). The relationship between competence and effectiveness is usually seen as a direct, causal relationship, so that speakers with reduced competence are seen as holding the responsibility for any decreased effectiveness of communication. When we recognise that messages are jointly constructed, competence can be seen as an emergent property of the exchange, rather than a quality residing in an individual (Wiemann and Bradac 1985). From this view, effectiveness in communication is achieved jointly through the contributions, adjustments and repairs of both partners. In the study of aphasia, this moves us from a deficit focus, where all communication breakdown is analysed in terms of aphasic error, toward a strength focus where we can begin to analyse not only the effect of aphasic difficulty on partner adjustments, but also the nature of the teamwork which enhances communication.

(3) *Aphasic/Normal/Normal Interaction*
     (28A(wife)/29NF(husband)/30NLF(daughter) Conversation, Tape 107 –118)

A   Yeah we got, ⎡ and we got
Husband   ⎣ And who did we call in and see?
A   We went and saw ah…um.. wh-,where do you always go that always (UNINTELLIGIBLE)
Husband   At Maclean
A   Ah oh yes, Maclean. We went and had had ah ah
Husband   Called and saw-
A   Ah..um
Daughter Bruce
A   Ah no not Bruce
Daughter Eve
A   Eve, ⎡ Eve, and their children and an
Husband   ⎣ Eve
A   And ah, also, um, the children, and also, ah um what's that girl's name? … um
Husband   Eve
A   Eve, Eve's ⎡ si-, ah mother
Husband   ⎣ /mʌ/-
Daughter Oh, that's right
A   And her husband were there
Daughter Mm, Alf
A   And ah, and er, and the two little.. ah.. ah
Daughter Dogs
A   Dogs (LAUGHS)

In Example 3, the three-way conversation between wife (aphasic), daughter and husband is a joint process, involving all three in the construction of the exchange. Both the daughter and the husband supply words (other-repair) for the aphasic individual, and the husband offers prompts to assist with the wife's word-finding difficulty (other initiated self-repair). While this example involves an aphasic speaker, this type of joint construction of the conversation is readily recognised as a normal feature of normal conversations, particularly those involving more than two speakers.

2.4 Judgement

Sociolinguistic perspectives issue a fundamental challenge to our judgements of effectiveness, which have been based traditionally on researcher-derived criteria, e.g. duration, accuracy. Such judgements have an undeserved reputation for objectivity, as can be seen when it is considered that researcher judgements require an assumption of speaker intent, inferences about listener understanding, and pre-determination of what aspects of communication are considered as significant to effectiveness (Eastwood 1988; Milroy 1987). Ethnomethodology offers an alternative way of studying effectiveness, as we can begin to ask how the participants themselves are judging the communication. Methods of doing this can involve asking the participants to reflect on past communication events, either directly from recordings or less directly through questionnaires or rating scales. Also, the methodology involving Conversation Analysis provides a further way of gaining insight into the participants' judgements, by drawing our attention to the evidence of understanding or misunderstanding which participants provide each other in the unfolding exchange.

So, for example, repair is observable evidence of one participant signalling trouble in the conversation (Schegloff, Jefferson and Sacks 1977; Van Lier 1988; Bremer, Broeder, Roberts, Simonot and Vasseur 1993). In this methodological framework it is important to recognise that even such signals need to be interpreted from the participant's point of view rather than the researcher's, so for example, a hesitant speaker may be signalling recognition of lower status through the manifestation of hesitancy, not necessarily a problem with message formulation (Jefferson 1975). The process of repair along its trajectories between speakers from turn to turn, allows for one way of obtaining an idea of the extent to which partners understand each other (or at least, of the extent to which partners are prepared to 'ride with' their present understanding). It is argued that this method of analysis involves a high degree of objectivity as it allows for explicit exposure of researcher interpretations, combined with high social validity in remaining close to participants' own judgements.

For example, in Example (3) above, we do not need to know the accuracy of the information being discussed, rather we can look to the responses of the participants to determine how acceptable the information is to them. So, the daughter explicitly confirms her understanding at one stage — 'that's right', while we know from the husband's prompts that he considers information needs correction — '/mʌ/'. We also know that the aphasic speaker was aware of difficulties through her explicit seeking for assistance — 'where do you....', and 'no not Bruce'.

2.5 Summary

To summarise thus far, we have considered a number of key elements which are considered essential for the description of the effectiveness of communication. Firstly, it has been argued that communication and its effectiveness need to be considered in terms of not only message content and accuracy, but also the effect on the interpersonal relationship, and the way language is used in the communication. Secondly, it has been argued that the analysis of processes by which communication is negotiated between speakers, enables consideration of how its effectiveness emerges. Thirdly, it has been suggested that effectiveness is a jointly produced outcome and so the contribution of all participants requires description. And finally, it has been suggested that the determination of the extent of effectiveness is made more validly through the consideration of the participants' judgements, rather than researchers' criteria. (See Figure 2 for summary).

3. Maximising Effectiveness

The goal of maximising communication effectiveness seems to be self-evidently valid, and yet frequently misses its intended target, due to insufficient specification. Part of the problem is that the term 'maximising' is as complex a combination of factors as that of effectiveness. When we say we are attempting to maximise effectiveness, we might be proposing to increase the quantity of any communication; or increasing the quantity of accurate communication; or improving the quality of the interaction through enhancement of existing resources in the context of situation (i.e. as part of the field, tenor and mode of the context); or providing new resources, e.g. augmentative channels of communication. We

Multilayered Description
(derived from Systemic Functional Linguistics, see Halliday & Hasan 1985)

Context	Field	Tenor	Mode
Metafunctions	Experiential	Interpersonal	Textual
Focus	Are messages doing what they set out to do?	How do they contribute to relationship?	How do they use resources of language?
Examples			
Situation	Message intent vs outcome	Power, status, harmony	Channel, cohesion
Culture	Type, amount, relevance	Politeness, familiarity	Lexical selection, density (style)

Dynamic Description
(derived from Conversational Analysis, see Schegloff, Jefferson & Sacks 1977)

Turntaking	progression and sequence # turns, turn length who holds the floor, and when?
Repair	self vs other correction prompts vs appeals for assistance patterns of repair: interactive, non-interactive

Evidence of participants' judgements of effectiveness
(see Schegloff 1992)

Overt comments *re* trouble understanding?
Overt comments *re* trouble producing message?
Other indicators (e.g. hesitancy, guessing, lack of uptake or continuation)

Responsibility
(see Ferguson 1996)

% of communication workload taken by each partner
| – – – – – – – 100% of communication – – – – – – – |

├───┤

speaker 1   speaker 2

Figure 2.   *Describing Communication Effectiveness*

equally might be seeking to increase/make use of/supply intra- and inter-individual processes which may make communication easier or faster (for either or both communication partners). We also may be seeking to make clients and partners more consciously aware of what they are doing already, or what they might try to do, which may facilitate effective communication. Clinically, to leave our goal for therapy articulated as simply 'maximising effectiveness of communication', grossly underspecifies what it is that we are trying to achieve.

This said, there is little in the available literature which can provide a systematic guide to ways in which goals for maximising communication effectiveness might be determined. The literature which is available has focussed traditionally on the development or reinforcement of what has been described as 'strategies' for communication. This body of work provides much commonsense and some empirical data upon which to build intervention, and will be discussed further, before going on to propose an alternative framework for systematically considering the resources which exist for using language strategically in order to maximise communication.

4.   Communication Strategies

In this section, the work on communication strategies in aphasia is grouped (roughly, and with apologies to any researcher who feels mis-placed!) according to the apparent underlying theoretical stance of the research. These groupings are described as 'clinical', 'holistic', 'behavioural', and 'linguistic'. It may be noted that the term 'pragmatic' has been avoided, mainly because much work described using this term falls across all four groupings.

4.1 Clinical

The work of Green (1982, 1984) provided an important impetus to the recognition of the importance of communication strategies in aphasia intervention. Green describes the importance of making use of significant contextual factors in both assessment and treatment and the potential value of incorporating speech act and discourse analysis in assessment and goal formulation for therapy. Green lists examples of a range of strategies which are familiar to any clinician working with the aphasic population, e.g. slow down rate, pause, use less ambiguous sentences, change topic, use alerters, place main words at the end of sentences, use short sentences, stress main words, use gesture, rephrase. Such advice often forms the basis of education provided to the communication partners of people with aphasia, e.g. in talks given to relatives, community groups, and handed out in pamphlet material. The limitations of the work which falls within this grouping is not its observational accuracy, but rather that to use such work appropriately depends heavily on the experience and insight which individual clinicians bring to the task. For example, there is no way of determing which strategies may be useful to try first, or with what sort of person (given both their aphasic difficulties and pre-morbid interaction styles).

4.2 *Holistic*

There is a paucity of work in the area of aphasia which addresses the problem through incorporating both consideration of the aphasic individual as a 'whole person', as well as recognition of the total environment and its effect on communication. Lubinski's (1994) work stands out in this respect. She considers aphasic individuals and their environments as related integrally, and that environmental changes may serve to promote improvements in communication. Her conception of environment encompasses the broader social and economic environment, the local physical environment, and the particular communication partners in the aphasic person's daily life. This approach provides tools which address the little explored areas of handicap (see Penn, this volume) in communication disorders.

Also within this grouping it is possible to consider Holland's (1980) description of performance on the test for Communicative Activities in Daily Living (CADL), a tool which addresses specific rather than general handicaps likely to be faced by aphasic individuals (see Penn, this volume). While the language sampling is derived rather than natural, the observational scoring involves holistic judgements, and the theoretical analysis of task construction and elicited performance allows for consideration of multiple factors making up the entire scenario enactments. Holistic approaches are recognised by most clinicians as clinically powerful, although so complex and multidimensional that research from this perspective continues to be limited. This complexity contributes also to the difficulties in identifying the interaction of environmental and individual factors in developing and using communication strategies. Holistic approaches to communication strategies can leave the clinician with that 'so what?' feeling — feeling that no greater insight was gained than could be derived from commonsense.

4.3 *Behavioural*

By far the most productive approach to providing empirical data about communication strategies has arisen from what is being described here as a 'behavioural' approach. Many diverse approaches are encapsulated by this grouping — it includes work from a strictly behaviour modification background (e.g. Goodkin, Diller and Shah 1973), as well as work from psycholinguistic perspectives which employ behavioural coding and categorisation as a means of describing key elements of what is being observed (e.g. work on cues, self-cues, and correction by such researchers as Marshall 1975; Marshall, Neuburger and Phillips 1994; Whitney and Goldstein 1989). Of particular interest for the purposes of this chapter, is the work which involves partners of aphasic individuals, e.g. work on strategies to improve comprehension through development of skills in requests for confirmation and clarification (Linebaugh, Margulies and Mackisack-Morin 1984). This behavioural grouping also includes the Edinburgh Functional Communication Profile (Skinner, Wirz, Thompson and Davidson 1984; Wirz, Skinner and Dean 1990), which describes key speech acts (e.g. responding, acknowledging) as well as other behaviours (e.g. problem solving). Most research in this grouping describes therapy which develops individualised communication strategies based on prior assessment to identify strategies which are present/ absent and facilitatory/non-facilitatory, e.g. Florance's (1981) Family Interaction Therapy; Newhoff and Apel's (1989) Significant Other training; Simmons, Kearns and Potechin (1987). Examples of the sorts of individualised strategies include reducing spouse interruption, reducing excessive use of convergent questions, cueing, and use of encouragers.

The strength of such work is its detailed and replicable methods of identifying and facilitating communication strategies. Such approaches provide a socially validated focus upon the disabilities faced by aphasic individuals within real world contexts, and so give some conception of potential handicaps and how they may be managed (see Penn, this volume). The difficulty with work within this grouping can be the lack of a systematic reason for target selection, i.e. while of course targeted strategies were entirely appropriate for the cases reported, they may or may not be as appropriate for other cases. Clinicians are left back with their clinical experience and commonsense for that selection.

4.4 *Linguistic*

While much of the research outlined above makes use of linguistic theory and analysis, the following approaches have been grouped together as they all require the integration of linguistic theory for their application, i.e. they cannot be used 'behaviourally'. They have in common also, a particular recourse to pragmatic theory and methods of analysis which are strongly influenced by ethno-methodology. Ethnomethodology is an approach to research which deliberately attempts to be theory-neutral, as the researcher attempts to approach observational data objectively and value-free in order to detect systematic and meaningful patterns of behaviour (Benson and Hughes 1983). Interpretation and theory are not neglected, but rather reserved for explict consideration once apparently significant patterns have been identified.

Lubinski, Duchan and Weitzner-Lin (1980) describe the identification of facilitatory and non-facilitatory strategies for a single case, e.g. hints and guesses, and they relate this to the agenda and shared knowledge of participants. A more generally applicable approach to therapy for communication strategies has been developed by Leiwo (1994) who describes working on such strategies as topic management (e.g. initiation, shifts) and problem management (e.g. clarification, negotiation of misunderstanding). A more specific focus on strategies for repair can be found in the work of Milroy and Perkins (1992) and Perkins (1995) who describe the complex moves involved in 'recycling' for repair, and Ferguson (1994) who discusses the possible effects of familiarity and activity on repair. Recent work reported by Simmons-Mackie and Damico (1997) describes individual interactional compensatory strategies using ethnomethodological procedures for analysis, and this work provides a socially valid estimate of handicap and directions for intervention at this level.

Such approaches to studying communication strategies have similar strengths to the above-described 'behavioural' approach, i.e. objectivity, replicability, and potential for therapeutic work. Yet the work described in this grouping has moved only partially beyond the identification of significant patterns of communication toward explicit systematic interpretation. Milroy and Perkins' (1992) work approaches this challenge as they relate observed patterns of repair to Clark and Schaefer's (1989) psycholinguistic model of interactive discourse. Also, as with the more 'behavioural' research, these approaches are not able to provide a systematic rationale for selection of communication strategies for therapy: the selection process is based on identification of presence/absence, and the clinician's judgement.

4.5   The Problem with 'Communication Strategies'

The limitations of the above research, from all perspectives, is not so much a reflection of the different methodologies used, but rather it is suggested that there are fundamental problems in the way communication strategies have been approached within the field of aphasia, and this is discussed in the following section.[3]

Briefly, the problems are these. Firstly, the term misleads us into thinking we are seeking to observe a unified behavioural pattern, when in fact what we observe is multifaceted and (to be effective) is changing constantly in response to what is going on in the communication exchange (Draper 1988). Secondly, how do we identify such patterns? By pattern do we simply mean a repeated set of behaviours? Does this mean that just because a strategy is employed only once that it is any less a strategy? Thirdly, what are our criteria for any specified behavioural set to be deemed a 'strategy'? Does, for example, the person using it (or involved in its use) have to be consciously aware of the set of behaviours as a strategy? If they do not, then what makes the use of communication strategies any different from any use of language? Bialystok (1990) argues that "Communication strategies ... are not aberrations, but part of normal language use" (p. vi). Is an alternative criterion that communication strategies must be goal directed? But again every use of language is goal directed, so what makes the use of communication strategies any different from any other use of language?

This last point is important in regard to communication strategies and aphasia, for we need to consider whether the use of communication strategies is being viewed as a resource available from the relatively intact pragmatic competence of the aphasic individual, i.e. are we seeing residual language function? For example, this appears to be the assumption in the work of Holland (1991) on conversational coaching. Alternatively, do communication strategies arise out of the adaptive processes of residual cognitive function (Kolk and Friederici 1985) — i.e. are we seeing a by-product of aphasia? Or, if we accept Bialystok's (1990) view that all use of language is 'strategic' in some sense, then are we seeing the damaged language system's 'best effort'?

There has been a tendency in the literature to view communication strategies as only associated with trouble in communication (see Coupland, Wiemann and Giles 1991 for a comprehensive discussion of this issue). Typically, so-called normal communication is seen as trouble-free, unproblematic, and strategies are what we bring into play to deal with communication breakdown. The ethno-methodological view of Conversation Analysis suggests otherwise. From this view, normal communication inherently is troubled, with each and every exchange involving strategic (as in 'purposeful') adjustments and negotiation of meaning. Communication breakdown may offer a highly observable window into both covert and overt strategies, but such strategic communication is the very essence of interaction. So, from this view, repair becomes the central strategic use of language. One way of conceptualising the relationship between strategies and communication behaviour in general, is to consider both repair and communication strategies as an integral subset of communication behaviours, with repair strategies acting retrospectively and other communication strategies acting preventively, i.e. prospectively.

5. Framework for Strategic Communication

Faerch and Kasper (1983 1984, 1986) working in the field of second language acquisition faced just these considerations in attempting to describe communication strategies of second language learners. They too face the difficulty of developing a descriptive system which is able to cope not only with the immense range and diversity of individual strategies, but also able to be useful in developing ways to teach such strategies. Rather than attempt a typology-based categorising of communication strategies[4] they propose a framework which highlights key options available for employing language strategically. An outline of this framework is represented in Figure 3.

   The framework presented incorporates work reported by Bremer, Broeder, Roberts, Simont and Vasseur (1993) which extends the options for productive linguistic strategies. In this framework, strategies are described as either 'productive' or 'receptive', in the sense that they facilitate the production or reception of the message. Some examples of each part of the framework are provided in Table 2[5] and a discussion of some of the more general features of the framework follows.

   Ferguson (1992a) proposes that it is useful to view receptive strategies as occurring on a continuum from indirect (e.g. 'wait and see') through direct (e.g. request for clarification) to directive (e.g. correction, instruction to repeat/rephrase). This end-point of the continuum concerns those receptive strategies where the listener directs the production of the speaker, and thus confirms reception of the message. Thus receptive strategies may require production on the part of the listener for their achievement. This interplay between receptive and productive strategies is seen also for productive strategies where messages are designed for the listener, and can involve checks on the understanding of the listener.

   The distinction between interactive and non-interactive production strategies indicates the extent to which the other partner is required for the achievement of the strategy. However, it should be noted, that in the sense that messages are designed for the listener, even the non-interactive strategies involve teamwork in the sense that they are affected by the other partner in the interaction.

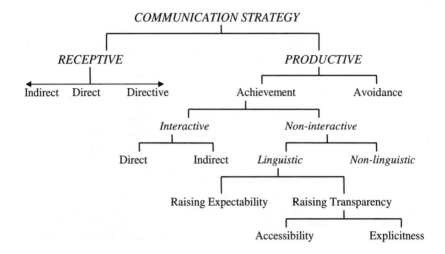

COMMUNICATION STRATEGY

RECEPTIVE   PRODUCTIVE

Indirect   Direct   Directive   Achievement   Avoidance

Interactive   Non-interactive

Direct   Indirect   Linguistic   Non-linguistic

Raising Expectability   Raising Transparency

Accessibility   Explicitness

Figure 3.   *Communication Strategy (based on the work of Faerch and Kasper 1984, 1986; Bremer et al. 1993)*

It is proposed that applying such a framework allows for a systematic 'top-down' approach to interpreting data originally obtained from the 'bottom-up' ethnomethodological approach. This has the advantage of maintaining the strengths of this latter approach, i.e. objectivity, replicability, validity, while allowing clinical and research use of a way of selecting and testing alternative strategies both for the one client and across clients. Further, it allows us to detail more specifically what we might be aiming for when we seek to maximise communication effectiveness. The implications of this and the other points raised in this chapter for the assessment and treatment of aphasia are discussed in the next section.

6.   Implications for Assessment

Much is already available in the aphasia literature which assists in the assessment of communication effectiveness, particularly from the work of those who have looked at the broader issues involved in functional communication and its rehabilitation for aphasia (see Manochiopinig, Sheard and Reed 1992 for a clinical review of pragmatic assessment). The present discussion focuses solely

Table 2. *Examples of Communication Strategies*

Strategy	Aphasic Individual	Normal Partner
Receptive — indirect	Repetition to aid own processing, to indicate trouble understanding	Acknowledge attention. Repetition to confirm. Allow time before respond.
Receptive — direct	Request repeat, clarification	Successive questions, guesses.
Receptive — directive	Ask other to slow down, to write it.	Conversational directive, tell to slow down. Request gesture, written, drawn, spelled response. Encourage use of Productive strategy. Provide cues.
Productive non-interactive non-linguistic	Gesture, mime, facial expression. Drawing. Tapping each syllable. Intonation. Delay.	Gesture, mime. Link gesture to topic start and end and main points. Pause, slow speech rate. Decrease dysfluency. Exaggerate stress.
Productive non-interactive linguistic	Interpret listener's lack of understanding Delay for silent rehearsal. Associations, synonyms, rhymes, opposites. Empty or general words. Self-correction, revision, approximation, restart. Self-question-cue, phrase triggers. Stereotypic context. Grapheme written, traced in air, first letter/word.	*Explicitness* Alter word choice, less ambiguous, less abstract, more specific. *Accessibility* Repeat, use more high frequency words. Chunk information. Reduce syntactic complexity. Write information down. *Expectability* Use verbal introducers, and terminators. Right-topic dislocation, give time to tune in, don't begin with key information.
Productive interactive indirect	Eye-gaze. Fillers, comment clauses. Watch other's face for placement cues.	Touch to alert, call name to alert.
Productive interactive direct	Ask other to wait, indicate need for time to respond. Request help.	Seek feedback as to whether understands. Tag questions.
Avoidance	Information deletion. Short turns. Use of direct speech	Information delection. Floor-holding.

on those particular implications raised by the issues presented in this chapter for assessment of communication effectiveness. The main implications relate to: scope, tools and goals of assessment.

6.1 Scope

All currently used assessments for aphasia provide some information which allows a view of the communication effectiveness of the person with aphasia. However, when the assessment of communication effectiveness is seen as the primary purpose of assessment (as opposed to, say, differential diagnosis, or determination of specific areas of cognitive-linguistic processing difficulty), then the issues raised in this chapter suggest that there are a number of key areas which require assessment. These have been previously summarised in Figure 1, which may provide guidance in describing communication effectiveness.

These guidelines suggest that assessment requires consideration of each main aspect (field, tenor, and mode) of significant contexts of situation for the individual, e.g. what the person talks about, with whom, and how. Those clinicians who work within theoretical perspectives other than Systemic Functional Linguistics may still find it useful to develop a broad description of how effectively the use of language conveys the message, contributes to the interpersonal relationship, and how coherently the message is expressed.

It is also suggested that the scope of assessment include consideration of the dynamic aspects of communication, e.g. turntaking, and repair. Clinicians who do not choose to employ the full range of Conversation Analysis methodology, may still find it useful to observe and describe their own observations of these aspects.

Assessment is enhanced by developing an understanding of how aphasic individuals and their communication partners view their communication effectiveness. So, the guidelines also suggest seeking their opinions with regard to 'who's doing the work' in the conversation. Research by Ferguson (1996) suggests that even people with severe aphasia are able and interested to provide an opinion about this, and that their judgements are usually very much in agreement with their communication partners' judgements.

These global judgements as to communication workload are worth comparing with the observation of the interactants' overt signals to each other during conversation with regard to understanding/misunderstanding. From this comparison, the clinician can begin to form a view of how the effectiveness of the communication is being managed.

6.2 *Tools*

Most of the assessment for communication effectiveness can be carried out within a one-hour clinical session. The depth of assessment is greatly enhanced if the client is able to bring along an audiotape recording of themselves in a number of short (5–10 minute) conversations with one or more significant communication partners. Home visits and observation in other settings (e.g. at self-help groups) increase the level of confidence that the assessment is based on valid sampling.

Many existing tools for assessment provide an appropriate base upon which to build, for example Holland's (1982) observational guidelines. The conversational frameworks outlined in Taylor (Sarno)'s (1965) Functional Communication Profile, Prutting and Kirchner's (1987) Pragmatic Protocol, and Penn's taxonomy of compensatory strategies (Penn 1987; Penn and Cleary 1988) are valuable guidelines for attempting to preserve the naturalism of interaction, while allowing for time-efficient data collection. The Revised Edinburgh Functional Communication Profile (Wirz, Skinner and Dean 1990) is an example of a more structured interaction, which still allows for observation of naturalistic communication. As previously mentioned, these tools are well suited to explorations of disability, and for preliminary considerations regarding handicap; however as discussed by Penn (this volume) the assessment of handicap is relatively underexplored.

Familiarity with the background and methodologies for using analyses based on Systemic Functional Linguistics (Halliday 1985; Eggins 1994) can take time to develop, and clinicians can feel that such fine-grain analysis may not yield sufficiently more insight to warrant the time spent. However, there are a number of ways to use these analyses clinically, for example by employing analyses on selected samples which are restricted in length, and by carrying out only those parts of analyses which appear pivotal to understanding the case at hand. Examples of productive analyses include: transitivity analyses to investigate how language is being used to 'do' things (see Mortensen 1992), analysis of Mood/Modality to investigate the expression of the interpersonal aspects of the relationship (see Ferguson 1992b), and cohesion analysis (see Armstrong 1991, 1993 for general discussion of using this analysis with aphasia).

The methodology of Conversation Analysis is often more accessible to clinicians, perhaps due to their background and experience with behavioural observation, and data recording. Transcription time is usually the most often reported barrier to the use of this methodology. However clinicians need to recognise that once significant patterns have been identified, that further observation often can be conducted 'on-line' (see Packman and Ingham 1978 for an interesting and still relevant discussion of this). Also, the use of selected sampling of key points of interaction can prove to be highly productive (see Ferguson 1994; Milroy and Perkins 1992; Perkins 1995).

6.3 Goals

While assessment in general may have many goals, assessment with regard to communication effectiveness is geared to identifying, selecting and developing specific therapy goals for maximising that communication effectiveness. As previously discussed, there is a need to think deeply and creatively about what exactly might be the specific goal.

One clinical trap is to 're-cycle' therapy goals, so that clients begin to receive therapy for only those goals with which the clinician has experience, or which have been reported in the empirical literature (for example, as taken from tables such as Table 1 above). One way of avoiding this trap is to incorporate ethnomethodological principles within the assessment, primarily the principle of approaching the data without prior assumptions as to what the interactants may be doing, or as to what might be more or less effective for that communication partnership. One example of this arose in the research by Ferguson (1994), where it had been assumed originally that 'other correction' would have negative consequences on the interaction (consistent with the often-given advice to relatives of aphasic individuals to not speak for or supply words for the person with aphasia). The conversational data revealed a different pattern entirely, where 'other correction' served to increase the speed and harmony of the conversational flow. The extent of diversity in repair patterns evidenced in the same research also serves as a warning to develop a detailed view of what the interactants are already doing, what works, and why. The therapy reported by Simmons, Kearns and Potechin (1987) is a good example of individualised and specific therapy goals for increasing communication effectiveness.

7. Implications for Treatment

As with assessment, there is much in the already available literature which is essential for providing therapy aimed at maximising communication effectiveness (see Strauss Hough and Pierce 1994 for a useful overview; and Holland 1991 for discussion of conversational intervention). The implications for treatment which arise from the issues discussed in this chapter relate to the following aspects of intervention: purpose, context, process, person, and outcome. Each of these aspects fundamentally relates to the discussion above of the development of goals for therapy, however in the following section these aspects are viewed as potentially manipulable variables in the ongoing process of implementing and refining a therapy program.

7.1 *Purpose*

Given the complex nature of 'effectiveness', it is important to attempt to clarify the underlying 'why' of therapy for this aspect of communication. This chapter has suggested previously that Faerch and Kasper's (1986) framework for describing strategic communication is particularly useful in this regard. Rather than identify and treat strategies aimed at increasing effectiveness solely because 'they're there', using this framework provides the clinician with a way of reflecting on just why a particular behavioural strategy may be useful, and hence with a systematic basis for selection.

So for example, a clinician may identify that a client's partner is using a 'wait and see' strategy when uncertain as to meaning, and that the client responds to this with increasingly off-topic tangential talk. Using the framework, we can consider the 'wait and see' strategy to be an indirect receptive strategy, which may be providing insufficient feedback for the client to initiate a more efficient productive strategy, such as an achievement, non-interactive, linguistic strategy to increase explicitness. The therapy may aim to promote the partner's use of more direct or directive receptive strategies (e.g. requesting clarification, asking the client to rephrase), with the underlying purpose being to promote the client's use of productive strategies.

Use of this framework not only allows for developing explicit rationales for selection of therapy, but also a way to evaluate its effects critically. In other words, rather than assuming that therapy is successful simply because the client or partner is now carrying out the specified behaviour, the success or otherwise of the therapy is judged by considering its effects on the interaction. So, in the example above, it may be that adoption of directive receptive strategies may have negative effects on the interaction, for example, the client may adopt avoidance strategies in response to perceived criticism. In such an event, the therapy does not achieve its purpose, although superficially its targetted behaviour has been achieved.

7.2 *Context*

Most guidelines for therapy aimed at increasing communication effectiveness view the different aspects of context as a source for generalisation activities following enstatement of the original communication strategy, e.g. through practice with different partners, and in different settings (see Davis and Wilcox 1985), and this is of course essential. However, the implications of the previously presented discussion of the aspects of context alert us to the potential use of each aspect of context in developing and refining therapy once the initial development of the therapy goal(s) has taken place.

For example, the initial formulation of the therapy for an aphasic individual may be to promote the use of appeals for assistance (direct, productive, interactive strategy). Consideration of key aspects of context may alert us to the need for ways to preserve 'face' and 'politeness' when seeking assistance, in order to maintain the harmony of the interpersonal relationship. Such consideration may help us reflect on what language resources the aphasic individual has available to them to manage this aspect, and while for some individuals the linguistic resources of the Mood system may be employed usefully (e.g. 'Do you think you might.....?'), others may need to employ alternative non-verbal channels (e.g. facial expression, hand gesture) to modulate such requests. Each aspect of context (field, tenor, mode) can be considered as a potential resource for supplementing and extending therapy.

7.3 *Process*

Perhaps because behavioural patterns are so easily observable, we can begin to think of them as 'things' or 'products' in themselves. The implication of previously discussed issues regarding the dynamic nature of communication, is that we need to stay aware of the process of communication, i.e. how the interactants are communicating strategically, rather than how they produce things called communication strategies.

For example, we may be working on reducing how often the communication partner interrupts the aphasic individual (i.e. which in this case arises from a non-interactive nonlinguistic strategy aimed at assisting the aphasic individual's production — albeit ineffectively). We need to be wary of developing the idea that we are working on a thing called 'turntaking', when in fact we are working on how the interactants manage to co-operate. The reason this is more than just a semantic distinction lies in how the development of the therapy occurs. If we are working just on 'turntaking', then we are able to promote a situation where both partners take an equal share of the floor. If we are working on the processes involved in developing closer teamwork in the communication, then turntaking becomes just one of the vehicles for achieving this.

7.4 *Person*

Once we recognise that communication is rarely a solitary event, then the implication is that therapy must involve communication partners. There are two main caveats to that statement however.

Firstly, 'involvement of the communication partner' is not achieved by their observer role in a client/clinician interaction. They are as much a part of the therapy process as the aphasic individual — part of the assessment, the goal, the implementation. Most examples of work with partners has tended to shift the focus from the client to the partner (e.g. Newhoff and Apel 1989), however the view being suggested here is that it is the *interaction* which is the focus of therapy. This means that there is a great deal of flexibility available in how goals are achieved, through one or other or both partners. Therapy provides ways in which the communication partners themselves can develop teamwork and the ability to adjust communication workload from moment to moment as the communication unfolds.

Secondly, it is recognised that in the elderly aphasic population it is not uncommon for a client to have no regular significant communication partners, i.e. most interactions may be short and involve exchange of goods and services, rather than interpersonally complex or involving substantive information giving. When this is the case, shifts may be required in the more usual therapist's role, integrating a greater use of conversational and interpersonal role-taking to develop the use of both interactive and non-interactive strategies by the aphasic individual (Laakso 1992; Sobiecka-Koszel 1991). A recent example of this type of approach, where the therapist deliberately moves into a less task-oriented and more partner-oriented role, has been reported by Murray and Holland (1995) whose data suggest the value of a 'conversational' approach with people who have acute aphasia.

7.5 *Outcome*

The implications of the views discussed in this chapter for the determination of outcome of therapy arise from the recognition of the validity of interactants' judgements with regard to communication effectiveness rather than those of outside observers (e.g. the therapist). The clinician will find the suggested methods of maximising the effectiveness of communication well-suited to behavioural measurement, and hence potentially available as data on service outcomes. However, it is important to note that change (or lack of change) in accordance with behavioural goals may not reflect necessarily the judgements of the participants in therapy.

So, for example, a partner may change a number of ways in which they communicate with their aphasic partner, yet find that the new style of interaction is interpersonally uncomfortable. Alternatively, no change may have been observable in the extent to which the aphasic individual and partner are able to increase the effectiveness of their communication, yet both partners may report a lessening of frustration and anxiety through having developed a 'meta-pragmatic' language with which to discuss the difficulties as they arise. In other words, it is important that therapy goals be specified clearly, and measured, in terms of the desired outcome for the interaction from the interactants' perspectives.

8. Conclusion

This chapter has presented a view in which the goal of maximising communication effectiveness is seen as requiring recognition of the multilayered and dynamic nature of how meanings are negotiated between communication partners. This view presents some guidelines for the scope of assessment and the ways in which therapy may be developed. In particular, this view suggests that communication effectiveness is a result, not a cause, of strategic communication. In line with this view, rather than therapy focussing on surface behavioural patterns, it needs to focus on underlying purposes of ways of using language in order to maximise effectiveness.

Notes

1. The empirical literature and examples presented in this chapter are drawn from the field of aphasia, however the general principles are applicable to other adult language disorders of neurological origin, e.g. cognitive-communication problems following head injury or dementia. It is also possible to apply the general principles to communication disorders involving a significant loss of intelligibility, e.g. child or adult dysarthria, hearing impairment, or adult laryngectomised speech, although specific examples will not apply. While of course parent-child interaction has its own specific features, clinicians working with carers of children with severe speech and language disorders may find the general principles to be a source of idea development.

2. The references cited here as examples of studies of aphasic repair are selected on the basis of analysing repair in natural conversation, and incorporating pragmatic theories in their methodol-

ogies and interpretation. There are, of course, many other studies of the phenomenon of repair in aphasia which have other purposes, e.g. Schlenck, Huber and Willmes' (1987) research into the monitoring for repair, and many other studies of repair in other communication disorders have employed experimental methodologies for eliciting repair, e.g. Brinton, Fujuki, Loeb and Winkler's (1986) study of the development of repair in children.

3. Much of the work which challenges traditional understandings of communication strategies has been done within the field of applied linguistics for second language acquisition, and many of the references given in the discussion of the problems with our conception of strategy are taken from this literature.

4. Taxonomies of communication strategies based on some sort of behavioural 'type' potentially face the same difficulty as previously discussed with reference to the identification and description of speech acts. Firstly, any one strategic use of communication may achieve multiple purposes, and secondly, any one purpose may involve multiple strategy 'types'. The resulting taxonomy potentially could be so large as to be unhelpful in providing either analysis of strategic communication or direction for therapy.

5. The examples presented in Table 2 are drawn from a wide range of published literature as well as pamphlet material distributed for relatives' information. Specific attribution of sources has not been made for each strategy, as each of these references discuss overlapping ranges of strategies, and combinations of strategies, though sometimes using different terminology. Interested readers will find these sorts of strategies discussed in the following works: Berman and Peelle (1967); Bugbee and Nichols (1980); Chiat and Gurland (1981); Flowers and Peizer (1984); Gerber and Gurland (1989); Goldblum (1985); Golper and Rau (1983); Green (1982 1984); LaPointe (1978); Linebaugh, Margulies and Mackisack-Morin (1984); Marshall (1975); Penn (1987); Skinner, Wirz, Thompson and Davidson (1984); and Ulatowska, Haynes, Hildebrand and Richardson (1977).

References

Armstrong, E. M. 1991. "The potential of cohesion analysis in the analysis and treatment of aphasic discourse". *Clinical Linguistics and Phonetics* 5 (1): 39–51.

Armstrong, E. M. 1993. "Aphasia rehabilitation: A sociolinguistic perspective". In *Aphasia Treatment: World Perspectives*, A. L. Holland and M. M. Forbes (eds). San Diego, CA: Singular.

Atkinson, J. M., and Heritage, J. (eds) 1984. *Structures of Social Action: Studies in Conversation Analysis*. Cambridge: Cambridge University Press.

Austin, J. L. 1975. *How to Do Things with Words* (2nd ed.). Oxford: Oxford University Press.

Benson, D., and Hughes, J. A. 1983. *The Perspective of Ethnomethodology*. London: Longman.

Berger, C. R., and Bradac, J. J. 1982. *Language and Social Knowledge: Uncertainty in Interpersonal Relations*. London: Edward Arnold.

Berman, M., and Peelle, L. 1967. "Self-generated cues: A method for aiding aphasic and apractic patients". *Journal of Speech and Hearing Disorders* 32: 372–6.

Berry, M. 1981. "Systemic linguistics and discourse analysis: A multilayered approach to exchange structure". In *Studies in Discourse Analysis*, C. Coulthard, and M. Montgomery (eds), 120–45. London: RKP.

Bialystok, E. 1990. *Communication Strategies: A Psychological Analysis of Second-Language Use*. Oxford: Basil Blackwell.

Boden, D., and Zimmerman, D.H. 1991. *Talk and Social Structure: Studies in Ethno-methodology and Conversation Analysis*. Cambridge: Polity Press.

Bremer, K., Broeder, P., Roberts, C., Simonot, M., and Vasseur, M. 1987. *Procedures Used to Achieve Understanding in a Second Language* (Final report to the Steering Committee of the European Science Foundation Additional Activity 'Second Language Acquisition by Adult Immigrants') London: European Science Foundation.

Bremer, K., Broeder, P., Roberts, C., Simonot, M., and Vasseur, M. 1993. "Ways of achieving understanding". In *Adult Language Acquisition: Cross-Linguistic Perspectives*, Perdue, C. (ed.). Cambridge: Cambridge University Press.

Brinton, B., Fujuki, M., Loeb, D., and Winkler, E. 1986. "Development of conversational repair strategies in response to requests for clarification". *Journal of Speech and Hearing Research* 29: 75–81.

Brown, P., and Levinson, S.C. 1987. *Politeness: Some Universals in Language Usage*. Cambridge: Cambridge University Press.

Bugbee, J.K., and Nichols, A.C. 1980. "Rehearsal as a self-correction strategy for patients with apraxia of speech". In *Clinical Aphasiology*, R.H. Brookshire (ed.). Minneapolis, MN: BRK Publishers.

Byng, S., and Black, M. 1989. "Some aspects of sentence production in aphasia". *Aphasiology* 3 (1): 241–263.

Chiat, S., and Gurland, G.B. 1981. "Comparative family perspectives on aphasia: Diagnosis, treatment, and counseling implications". In *Clinical Aphasiology*, R.H. Brookshire (ed.). Minneapolis, MN: BRK Publishers.

Clark, H.H., and Schaefer, E.F. 1989. "Contributing to discourse". *Cognitive Science* 13: 259–294.

Clark, H., and Wilkes-Gibbs, D. 1986. "Referring as a collaborative process". *Cognition* 22: 1–39.

Coltheart, M. 1987. "Functional architecture of the language-processing system". In *The Cognitive Neuropsychology of Language*, M. Coltheart, G. Sartori, and R. Job (eds), Chapter 1. London: Lawrence Erlbaum.

Coulthard, M. 1985. *An Introduction to Discourse Analysis* (2nd ed.). London: Longman.

Coupland, N., Wiemann, J.M., and Giles, H. 1991. "Talk as 'problem' and communication as 'miscommunication': An integrative analysis". In *"Miscommunication" and Problematic Talk*, N. Coupland, H. Giles, and J.M. Wiemann (eds), Chapter 1. Newbury Park, CA: Sage.

Davis, G.A., and Wilcox, M.J. 1985. *Adult Aphasia Rehabilitation: Applied Pragmatics*. San Diego, CA: College-Hill.

Draper, S. W. 1988. "What's going on in everyday explanation?". In *Analysing Everyday Explanations: A Casebook of Methods*, C. Antaki (ed.). London: Sage.

Duffy, J. R. 1994. "Schuell's stimulation approach to rehabilitation". In *Language Intervention Strategies in Adult Aphasia*, R. Chapey (ed.), Chapter 7. Baltimore, MD: Williams and Wilkins.

Duncan, S. 1975. "Interaction units during speaking turns in dyadic, face-to-face conversations". In *Organization of Behavior in Face-to-Face Interaction*, A. Kendon, R. M. Harris, and M. R. Key (eds). The Hague: Mouton.

Eastwood, J. 1988. "Qualitative research: An additional research methodology for speech pathology?". *British Journal of Disorders of Communication* 23: 171–184.

Eggins, S. 1994. *An Introduction to Sytemic Functional Linguistics*. London: Pinter.

Faerch, C., and Kasper, G. (eds) 1983. *Strategies in Interlanguage Communication*. London: Longman.

Faerch, C., and Kasper, G. 1984. "Two ways of defining communicative strategies". *Language Learning* 34 (1): 45–65.

Faerch, C., and Kasper, G. 1986. "Strategic competence in foreign language teaching". In *Learning, Teaching and Communication in the Foreign Language Classroom*, G. Kasper (ed.). Aarhus: Aarhus University Press.

Ferguson, A. 1992a. *Conversational Repair in Aphasic and Normal Interaction*. Unpublished Ph.D. Thesis, Macquarie University, Sydney.

Ferguson, A. 1992b. "Interpersonal aspects of aphasic conversation". *Journal of Neurolinguistics* 7 (4): 277–294.

Ferguson, A. 1994. "The influence of aphasia, familiarity, and activity on conversational repair". *Aphasiology* 8 (2): 143–157.

Ferguson, A. 1996. "Describing competence in aphasic/normal conversation". *Clinical Linguistics and Phonetics* 10 (1): 55–63.

Florance, C. L. 1981. "Methods of communication analysis used in family interaction therapy". In *Clinical Aphasiology*, R. H. Brookshire (ed.), 204–211. Minneapolis, MN: BRK Publishers.

Flowers, C. R., and Peizer, E. R. 1984. "Strategies for obtaining information from aphasic persons". In *Clinical Aphasiology*, R. H. Brookshire (ed.), 106–113. Minneapolis, MN: BRK Publishers.

Gerber, S., and Gurland, G. B. 1989. "Applied pragmatics in the assessment of aphasia". *Seminars in Speech and Language* 10 (4): 263–281.

Goldblum, G. M. 1985. "Aphasia: A societal and clinical appraisal of pragmatic and linguistic behaviours". *Die Suid-Afrikaanse Tydskrif vir Kommunikasieafwykings* 32: 11–18.

Golper, L. A. C., and Rau, M. T. 1983. "Systematic analysis of cuing strategies in aphasia: Taking your 'cue' from the patient". In *Clinical Aphasiology*, R. H. Brookshire (ed.). Minneapolis, MN: BRK Publishers.

Goodkin, R., Diller, L, and Shah, N. 1973. "Training spouses to improve the functional speech of aphasic patients". In *The Modification of Language Behavior*, B. B. Lahey (ed.), Chapter 6. Springfield, ILL: Charles C. Thomas.

Goodwin, C. 1981. *Conversational Organization: Interaction between Speakers and Hearers*. New York, NY: Academic Press.

Green, G. 1982. "Assessment and treatment of the adult with severe aphasia: Aiming for functional generalisation". *Australian Journal of Human Communication Disorders* 10: 11–23.

Green, G. 1984. "Communication in aphasia therapy: Some of the procedures and issues involved". *British Journal of Disorders of Communication* 19: 35–46.

Grice, H. 1975. "Logic and conversation". In *Syntax and Semantics, vol.3: Speech Acts*, P. Cole, and J. L. Morgan (eds), 41–58. New York, NY: Academic Press.

Grimshaw, A. 1980. "Mishearings, misunderstandings and other nonsuccesses in talk: A plea for redress of a speaker-oriented bias". *Sociological Inquiry* 50: 31–74.

Grodzinsky, Y. 1988 "Unifying the various language-related sciences: Aphasic syndromes and grammatical theory". In *Theoretical Linguistics and Disordered Language*, M. J. Ball (ed.). London: Croom Helm.

Halliday, M. A. K. 1978. *Language as Social Semiotic*. Sydney: Edward Arnold.

Halliday, M. A. K. 1985. *An Introduction to Functional Grammar*. London: Edward Arnold.

Halliday, M. A. K., and Hasan, R. 1976. *Cohesion in English*. London: Longman.

Halliday, M. A. K., and Hasan, R. 1985. *Language, Context and Text: Aspects of Language in a Social-Semiotic Perspective*. Victoria: Deakin University Press.

Halliday, M. A. K., and Plum, G. 1985. "On casual conversation". In *Discourse on Discourse* (Occasional papers No. 7), R. Hasan (ed.). Applied Linguistics Association of Australia.

Hammersley, M., and Atkinson, D. 1983. *Ethnography: Principles in Practice*. London: Tavistock.

Harley, T. A. 1993. "Connectionist approaches to language disorders". *Aphasiology* 7 (3): 221–249.

Holland, A. L. 1980. *Communicative Abilities in Daily Living (CADL): A Test of Functional Communication*. Baltimore: University Park Press.

Holland, A. L. 1982. "Observing functional communication of aphasic adults". *Journal of Speech and Hearing Disorders* 47: 50–56.

Holland, A. L. 1991. "Pragmatic aspects of intervention in aphasia". *Journal of Neurolinguistics* 6 (2) 197–211.

Jefferson, G. 1975 "Error correction as an interactional resource". *Language in Society* 3: 181–199.

Kolk, H. J., and Friederici, A. D. 1985. "Strategy and impairment in sentence understanding by Broca's and Wernicke's aphasics". *Cortex* 21 (1): 47–67.

Laakso, M. 1992. "Interactional features of aphasia therapy conversations". *Studies in Logopedics and Phonetics* 3 (4): 69–90.

Lantolf, J. P., and Frawley, W. 1988. "Proficiency: Understanding the construct". *Studies in Second Language Acquisition* 10 (2): 181–195.

LaPointe, L. 1978. "Aphasia therapy: Some principles and strategies for treatment". In *Clinical Managment of Neurogenic Communicative Disorders*, D. F. Johns (ed.). Boston: Little, Brown and Co.

Leech, G. 1983. *Principles of Pragmatics*. London: Longman.

Leiwo, M. 1994. "Aphasia and communicative speech therapy". *Aphasiology* 8(5): 467–506.

Linebaugh, C. W., Margulies, C. P., and Mackisack-Morin, E. L. 1984. "The effectiveness of comprehension-enhancing strategies employed by spouses of aphasic patients". In *Clinical Aphasiology*, R. H. Brookshire (ed.), 188–197. Minneapolis, MN: BRK Publishers.

Lubinski, R. 1994. "Environmental systems approach to adult aphasia". In *Language Intervention Strategies in Adult Aphasia*, R. Chapey, (ed.), Chapter 13. Baltimore, MD: Williams and Wilkins.

Lubinski, R., Duchan, J., and Weitzner-Lin, B. 1980. "Analysis of breakdowns and repairs in aphasic adult communication". In *Clinical Aphasiology*, R. H. Brookshire (ed.), 111–116. Minneapolis, MN: BRK Publishers.

Manochiopinig, S., Sheard, C., and Reed, V. 1992. "Pragmatic assessment in adult aphasia: A clinical review". *Aphasiology* 6 (6): 519–533.

Marshall, J. 1995. "The mapping hypothesis and aphasia therapy". *Aphasiology* 9 (6): 517–541.

Marshall, R. C. 1975. "Word retrieval strategies of aphasic adults in conversational speech". In *Clinical Aphasiology*, R. H. Brookshire (ed.), 278–284. Minneapolis, MN: BRK Publisher.

Marshall, R. C., Neuburger, S. I., and Phillips, D. S. 1994. "Verbal self-correction and improvement in treated aphasic clients". *Aphasiology* 8 (6): 535–547.

Martin, J. R. 1987. "The meaning of features of systemic linguistics". In *New Developments in Systemic Linguistics: vol.1: Theory and Description*, M. A. K. Halliday and R. P. Fawcett (eds). London: Pinter.

Martin, J. R. 1992. *English Text: System and Structure*. Amsterdam: Benjamins.

Milroy, L. 1987. *Observing and Analysing Natural Language: A Critical Account of Sociolinguistic Method*. Oxford: Basil Blackwell.

Milroy, L., and Perkins, L. 1992. "Repair strategies in aphasic discourse: Toward a collaborative model". *Clinical Linguistics and Phonetics* 6 (1,2): 27–40.

Mortensen, L. 1992. "A transitivity analysis of discourse in dementia of the Alzheimer's type". *Journal of Neurolinguistics* 7 (4): 309–321.

Murray, L. L., and Holland, A. L. 1995. "The language recovery of acutely aphasic patients receiving different therapy regimens". *Aphasiology* 9 (4): 397–405.

Newhoff, M., and Apel, K. 1989. "Environmental communication programming with aphasic persons". *Seminars in Speech and Language* 10(4): 315–328.

Ochs, E. and Schieffelin, B.B. (eds) 1979. *Developmental Pragmatics*. New York: Academic Press.

Packman, A. and Ingham, R.J. 1978. "On-line measurement of aphasic speech". *Perceptual and Motor Skills* 47: 851–856.

Penn, C. 1987. "Compensation and language recovery in the chronic aphasic patient". *Aphasiology* 1 (3): 235–245.

Penn, C., and Cleary, J. 1988. "Compensatory strategies in the language of closed head injured patients". *Brain Injury* 2 (1): 3–17.

Perkins, L. 1995. "Applying conversation analysis to aphasia: Clinical implications and analytic issues". *European Journal of Disorders of Communication* 30 (3): 372–383.

Porch, B. 1994. "Treatment of aphasia subsequent to the Porch Index of Communicative Abilty (PICA)". In *Language Intervention Strategies in Adult Aphasia*, R. Chapey (ed.), Chapter 8. Baltimore, MD: Williams and Wilkins.

Prutting, C.A., and Kirchner, D.M. 1987. "A clinical appraisal of the pragmatic aspects of language". *Journal of Speech and Hearing Disorders* 52 (2): 105–119.

Sacks, H., Schegloff, E., and Jefferson, G. 1974. "A simplest systematics for the organization of turn taking for conversation". *Language* 50: 696–735.

Schegloff, E.A. 1992. "Repair after next turn: The last structurally provided defense of intersubjectivity in conversation". *The American Journal of Sociology* 97 (5): 1295–1345.

Schegloff, E.A., Jefferson, G., and Sacks, H. 1977. "The preference for self-correction in the organization of repair in conversation". *Language* 53: 361–382.

Schlenck, K., Huber, W., and Willmes, K. 1987. "'Prepairs' and repairs: Different monitoring functions in aphasic language production". *Brain and Language* 30: 226–244.

Searle, J.R. 1969. *Speech Acts: An Essay in the Philosophy of Language*. London: Cambridge University Press.

Simmons, N.N., Kearns, K.P., and Potechin, G. 1987. "Treatment of aphasia through family member training". In *Clinical Aphasiology*, R.H. Brookshire (ed.). Minneapolis, MN: BRK Publishers.

Simmons-Mackie, N.N. and Damico, J.S. 1997. "Reformulating the definition of compensatory strategies in aphasia". *Aphasiology* 11 (8): 761–781.

Skinner, C., Wirz, S., Thompson, I., and Davidson, J. 1984. *Edinburgh Functional Communication Profile* (1st ed.). Buckingham: Winslow Press.

Sobiecka-Koszel, G. 1991. "Communication strategies: The therapist as the dominant partner". *Aphasiology* 5 (2): 197–199.

Strauss Hough, M., and Pierce, R.S. 1994. "Pragmatics and treatment". In *Language Intervention Strategies in Adult Aphasia*, R. Chapey, (ed.), Chapter 12. Baltimore, MD: Williams and Wilkins.

Sperber, D., and Wilson, D. 1986/1995. *Relevance: Communication and cognition* (1st/2nd ed.). Oxford: Basil Blackwell.

88   ALISON FERGUSON

Stubbs, M. 1983. *Discourse Analysis: The Sociolinguistic Analysis of Natural Language*. Oxford: Basil Blackwell.
Taylor (Sarno), M. 1965. "A measurement of functional communication in aphasia". *Archives of Physical Medicine and Rehabilitation* 46: 101–7.
Togher, L., Code, C., and Hand, L. 1995. "Analysis of discourse in the closed head injured population". Paper presented at the Clinical Aphasiology Conference, Sunriver, Oregon.
Ulatowska, H. K., Haynes, S. M., Hildebrand, B. H., and Richardson, S. M. 1977. "The aphasic individual: A speaker and a listener, not a patient". In *Clinical Aphasiology*, R. H. Brookshire (ed.), 198–213. Minneapolis, MN: BRK Publishers.
Van Dijk, T. A. 1981. *Studies in the Pragmatics of Discourse*. Mouton: The Hague.
Werth, P. 1984. *Focus, Coherence and Emphasis*. London: Croom-Helm.
Wiemann, J. M., and Bradac, J. J. 1985. "The many guises of communicative competence". *Journal of Language and Social Psychology*, 4 (2): 131–8.
Van Lier, L. 1988. *The Classroom and the Language Learner: Ethnography and Second Language Classroom Research*. London: Longman.
Wilcox, J., and Davis, G. A. 1977. "Speech act analysis of aphasic communication in individual and group settings". In *Clinical Aphasiology*, R. H. Brookshire (ed.), 166–74. Minneapolis, MN: BRK Publisher.
Wirz, S. L., Skinner, C., and Dean, E. 1990. *Revised Edinburgh Functional Communication Profile (EFCP)* (2nd ed.) Tucson, AZ: Communication Skill Builders.
Whitney, J. L., and Goldstein, H. 1989. "Using self-monitoring to reduce dysfluencies in speakers with mild aphasia". *Journal of Speech and Hearing Disorders* 54: 576–86.

Problems of Pragmatic Profiling

Martin J. Ball
University of Ulster

1. Introduction

There has, of course, long been an interest in the function of language as well as the structure of language, but it has only been in the last dozen years or so that we have seen the widespread influence of the area of communication that has been termed pragmatics. The late seventies saw the start of publication of a journal devoted to the area, and in more recent times several major texts on pragmatics have appeared (Leech 1983, Levinson 1983, Mey 1993, Grundy 1995 and Verschueren, Östman and Blommaert 1995).

It is not necessary to enter the debate here as to the scope of the term pragmatics (see for example Levinson, 1983), or indeed its relationship to other areas of linguistics (what McTear and Conti-Ramsden 1989, after Craig 1983, have termed the narrow and broad views of pragmatics). Instead, we want to look at the application of pragmatics to the clinical linguistic situation.

In recent times there has been a big increase in the study of the relationship between pragmatics and disordered language. This can been seen, for example, in the work reported in Gallagher and Prutting (1983), Grunwell and James (1989), McTear and Conti-Ramsden (1989) and Lesser and Milroy (1993), as well as in numerous papers published in collections (for example Smith 1988) and in the speech pathology journals (see McTear and Conti-Ramsden for accounts of some of these). Much of this work has been devoted to aspects of the assessment of pragmatics in the speech/language pathology clinic. As McTear and Conti-Ramsden (1989) have pointed out, these assessment procedures (as with other areas of linguistic inquiry) tend to fall into two broad categories: standardised tests, and 'pragmatic checklists' or profiles.

There has been some debate in the speech pathology literature in the past on the respective merits of these two approaches (see for example, Crystal, Fletcher

and Garman 1976, and Müller, Munro and Code 1981) which we will not pursue
further here. For the purposes of this account, however, we will take the view
that the linguistic profile is likely to provide a full picture of the area of language being assessed, and could well provide also a principled approach to
remediation.

In clinical pragmatic assessment the main emphasis appears to have been on
children with speech/language disorders. For example, Bates (1976) and McTear
(1985) examine the acquisition of pragmatics by children, Smith (1988) concentrates her discussion on pragmatics in children, and many of the contributions to
Gallagher and Prutting (1983) deal with speech/language disordered children.
McTear and Conti-Ramsden (1989) provide a bibliography of such work,
including work of their own. Several profiles are noted in this literature as being
designed for use with children: Roth and Spekman (1984a,b), McTear (1985),
Bedrosian (1985), Prutting and Kirchner (1983, 1987), and Dewart and Summers
(1988). It can be argued, of course, whether all of these are genuinely profiles,
or whether they adopt too broad or too narrow a definition of pragmatics, but
that is a discussion for elsewhere. We have also excluded from consideration
other assessments of 'functional ability' (e.g. FCP, Sarno 1969; EFCP, Skinner,
Wirz, Thompson, and Davidson 1984), although recognising their link with
current work.

The assessment of pragmatic abilities in aphasics has been until recently a
relatively neglected area in comparison with the work on children. It is partly
because of this, perhaps, that we have been attracted to this aspect of pragmatic
assessment for this account. In particular we want to examine the Pragmatic
Protocol of Prutting and Kirchner, which the authors note can be used both with
children and with adults, and the Profile of Communicative Appropriateness,
designed by Claire Penn (1988) specifically for use with aphasics. Manochiopinig, Sheard and Reed (1992) did undertake a review of a wide range of
pragmatic assessment tools for adult aphasia but, unfortunately, this study was
more descriptive than critical, and fails to look in detail at the problems of
utilising the various approaches it chronicles. It is, however, a good source of
reference to the range of pragmatic assessments for adults that have been
proposed.

In examining such profiles, we can investigate four aspects of assessing
pragmatics: the consistency of scorers, the difference between two-point and
five-point scales, the ability of the profiles to distinguish between different
aphasic syndromes, and their usefulness in planning remediation (this last area is
discussed in detail in Davies and Wilcox 1985). We also wanted to examine
briefly the ease (or otherwise) of operation of the profiles. In the experiment

described below we discuss results of a preliminary enquiry, concentrating on the first two of these aspects.

The reasons for looking at these points is that pragmatic assessment, unlike for example syntactic assessment, is a much less concrete activity. Whereas the syntactic labelling of an utterance in the LARSP procedure (Crystal, Fletcher and Garman 1976) is something that is generally not open to debate, the acceptability or otherwise of a particular pragmatic behaviour is not so clear-cut, and may depend on the assessor, or the delicacy of the scoring mechanism; both factors affecting the usefulness of the profile as a diagnostic tool and a guide to intervention.

In order to illustrate this point further, we can consider some examples highlighting the different approach needed to syntactic and pragmatic material. Consider the following utterance produced by a language-impaired speaker:

(1)   it's a lovely sunny day

We can submit this utterance to a syntactic analysis following the LARSP conventions, and we arrive at a three-level labelling as follows:

(2)   It' s   a lovely sunny day
       S V   C   (clause level)
       it cop D Adj   Adj N   (phrase level)
         'cop   (word level)

Anyone trained in the grammatical terminology used in this profile will arrive at this same labelling: it is not open to subjective interpretation. Naturally, the grammatical framework employed in LARSP may well be challenged; for example, whether a division between clause and phrase level is psycholinguistically well-motivated, whether a distinction between object and complement is purely syntactic rather than semantic, and so on. But that is not what is at issue here: given this framework, all clinical linguists will reach the same analysis. Further, if the utterance had contained syntactic errors (such as omissions, wrong ordering of elements, etc.), these too would have been unambiguously classifiable in LARSP terms.

We can extend the argument into phonology. Suppose (1) above had been pronounced as follows:

(3)   it's a lovely sunny day
       [ɪtθ ə jʌvji θʌni deɪ]

Anyone trained in phonetics and phonology will be able to identify the differences between a target pronunciation for that utterance, and the subject's realisation. The two general differences involve the use of a dental fricative for the target alveolar, and the use of a palatal approximant for the target alveolar lateral. No other analysis is possible, again it is not open to subjective interpretation. Certainly, the way in which one characterises these two features is open to theoretical debate; it may be in terms of features, rules, processes or non-linear formalisms. However, these competing theoretical mechanisms would have been building on an agreed data set.

In pragmatic analysis, however, things are not so simple. Let us return to example (1). Out of context, this appears a perfectly normal utterance. Nevertheless, one can easily envisage circumstances when it will seem pragmatically decidedly odd. In the following dialogue, for example, it would not be expected:

> (4)   A: What time is it?
>   B: It's a lovely sunny day

In such circumstances, we would be inclined to mark B's reply as being pragmatically unacceptable (by, among other things, breaking Gricean maxims on conversation). We might, however, wish to modify degrees of unacceptability if we compare (4) with (5):

> (5)   A: What time is it?
>   C: There are green cows over there

Degrees of unacceptable pragmatic behaviour are, however, bound to be subjective as an infinite range of odd utterances may occur and different analysts may well come to different conclusions. If we compare the following two replies to the time question, we might be hard pressed to decide which is more or less acceptable:

> (6)   A: What time is it?
>   B: It's a lovely sunny day
>   A: What time is it?
>   D: What the clock says

While B's answer appears to violate semantic links, D's clearly sounds as if it is breaking links of politeness (though that may not be the underlying 'cause' for this reply).

Further, knowledge of context is very important in attempting pragmatic classifications. Let us consider the following exchange:

> (7)   A: What time is it?
>   E: It's just gone midnight

At first sight, E's reply might well be classed as perfectly acceptable. But, if the time happens to be mid-morning, then E's reply would surely be more unacceptable than B's. Indeed, if B has problems manipulating the number system or specifically applying it to telling the time, the reply "it's a lovely sunny day" may well be B's attempt to indicate an appropriate reply to the request about time through indicating that it's the time when the sun is out. In other words, what may be inappropriate pragmatic behaviour for an unimpaired speaker may well be appropriate avoidance or compensatory behaviour for a language impaired speaker.

What we have attempted to show, then, is that pragmatic analysis — at least in terms of scoring behaviours — is difficult and subjective. It will not lead to such clear-cut results as found with other levels of linguistic behaviour. Further, we need not only be careful about how pragmatic behaviours are classed in terms of other behaviours, but we also need to know what we are judging them against overall: 'normal' pragmatic behaviour, or that appropriate for a speaker with a specific disorder.

2.   The Pragmatic Protocol

The Pragmatic Protocol was designed by Prutting and Kirchner (1983), and is used here in its revised form of 1987. It is shown in Figure 1. As can be seen it consists of thirty pragmatic parameters, divided into 7 groups, which in turn are assigned to three 'aspects': verbal, paralinguistic, and non-verbal. The authors provide specific guidance on assigning behaviours to either of the two main marking categories: appropriate or inappropriate (a 'no opportunity to observe' category is also available). This guidance is as follows:

> Appropriate. Parameters are marked appropriate if they are judged to facilitate the communicative interaction or are neutral. Inappropriate. Parameters are marked inappropriate if they are judged to detract from the communicative exchange and penalize the individual. (Prutting and Kirchner 1987: 108).

The study reported in Prutting and Kirchner (1987) also reports on inter-scorer reliability (ranging between 91% and 100% for various groups of subjects); and on typical profiles for different language disorders. We will return to this last point briefly later.

3. Profile of Communicative Appropriateness

This profile was devised by Penn (1988), based on earlier work (Penn 1983). This profile was specifically designed for work with aphasics, and follows closely the analysis of pragmatics proposed in Levinson (1983). The profile chart is shown in Figure 2. The fifty or so parameters are grouped in six main sections: response to interlocutor, control of semantic content, cohesion, fluency, sociolinguistic sensitivity, and non-verbal communication.

The profile also requires a marking system using a five point scale: inappropriate, mostly inappropriate, some appropriate, mostly appropriate, appropriate, with a 'could not evaluate' category as well. This system clearly adds sensitivity to the analysis, but likewise could add to the difficulty in inter-scorer reliability. Statistical analysis reported in Penn (1988) suggests inter-scorer reliability in her investigation was good. She also reports on the diagnostic ability of the PCA, and we return briefly to this subject later.

4. The Study

An initial study on this area was described in Ball, Davies, Duckworth and Middlehurst (1991). The main features of that experiment are reported again below. This investigation was designed to assess reliability in pragmatic profiling, but was deliberately constructed to manipulate extremes; that is to say, the profiles were chosen to be as different as possible in terms of their scoring methods (though not necessarily in terms of pragmatic behaviours to be assessed), and the raters to be as different as possible in terms of their backgrounds. Such a design will clearly highlight potential problems in as economical a way as possible; however, we have to remember that it will also exaggerate such problems which in the clinical situation may well be mitigated through adequate training and preparation. We return to this point later in the chapter.

4.1 *Method*

4.1.1 *Subjects*
Two aphasic subjects were chosen for this investigation. Mrs T., then aged 47, suffered a left-hemisphere cva in December 1979, located in the temporal lobe, resulting in right hemiplegia. A variety of assessments indicated a Broca's type aphasia. Comprehension was slightly impaired, with expression showing agrammatism. Slight apraxia of speech was noted. Reading was severely impaired, with

PRAGMATIC PROFILE

NAME: _____   DATE: _____
COMMUNICATIVE   COMMUNICATIVEPARTNER'S
SETTINGOBSERVED _____   RELATIONSHIP_____

Communicative act	Appropriate	Inappropriate	No opportunity to observe	Examples and comments
Verbal aspects				
A. Speech Acts				
1. Speech act pair analysis				
2. Variety of speech acts				
B. Topic				
3. Selection				
4. Introduction				
5. Maintenance				
6. Change				
C. Turn taking				
7. Initiation				
8. Response				
9. Repair/revision				
10. Pause time				
11. Interruption/ overlap				
12. Feedback to speakers				
13. Adjacency				
14. Contingency				
15. Quantity/ conciseness				
D. Lexical selection/ use across speech acts				
16. Specificity/ accuracy				
17. Cohesion				
E. Stylistic variations				
18. The varying of communicative style				
Paralinguistic aspects				
F. Intelligibility and prosodics				
19. Intelligibility				
20. Vocal intensity				
21. Vocal quality				
22. Prosody				
23. Fluency				
Nonverbal aspects				
G. Kenesics and proxemics				
24. Physical proximity				
25. Physical contacts				
26. Body posture				
27. Foot/leg and hand/arm movements				
28. Gestures				
29. Facial expression				
30. Eye gaze				

Figure 1.   *The Pragmatic Protocol*

PROFILE OF COMMUNICATIVE APPROPRIATENESS

Name _____   Features of sampling _____

Date _____   Unit of analysis _____

Person eliciting sample _____

		I	II	III	IV	V	VI	COMMENTS
Response to interlocutor	Request							
	Reply							
	Clarification request							
	Acknowledgement							
	Teaching probe							
	Others							
Control of semantic content	Topic initiation							
	Topic adherence							
	Topic shift							
	Lexical choices							
	Idea completion							
	Idea sequencing							
	Others							
Cohesion	Ellipsis							
	Tense use							
	Reference							
	Lexical substitution forms							
	Relative clauses							
	Prenominal adjectives							
	Conjunctions							
	Others							
Fluency	Interjections							
	Repetitions							
	Revisions							
	Incomplete phrases							
	False starts							
	Pauses							
	Word-finding difficulties							
	Others							
Sociolinguistic sensitivity	Polite forms							
	Reference to interlocutor							
	Placeholders, fillers, stereotypes							
	Acknowledgements							
	Self correction							
	Comment clauses							
	Sarcasm/humour							
	Control of direct speech							
	Indirect speech acts							
	Others							
Non-verbal Communication	Vocal aspects. Intensity							
	Pitch							
	Rate							
	Intonation							
	Quality							
	Non-verbal aspects: Facial expression							
	Head movement							
	Body posture							
	Breathing							
	Social distance							
	Gesture and pantomime							
	Others							
	TOTALS							

Key: I. Inappropriate; II. Mostly inappropriate; III. Some appropriate; IV. Mostly appropriate; V. Appropriate; VI. Could not evaluate.

Figure 2.   *The Profile of Communicative Appropriateness*

writing reflecting the deficits in language output. Pragmatic aspects of communication were described by the clinician as being appropriate in many respects, with non-verbal behaviour being used to compensate for limited language output, good self-monitoring, and good use of repair strategies.

Mr D. suffered a left, posterior cva in June 1982, resulting in right hemiplegia. He was then aged 69. Initial assessments indicated a Wernicke's type aphasia with severely impaired comprehension, but fluent expression albeit with some jargon aphasia. Reading was severely impaired, and the only writing task accomplished was copying. Pragmatic skills were reported as being severely impaired, with poor self-monitoring, no awareness of turn-taking or repair strategies. The initial deficits have resolved somewhat, and Mr D. has improved self-awareness, repetition ability and sentence completion. Recent assessments suggest that his problems are now better characterised as transcortical sensory aphasia.

The subjects were both recorded on video in May 1989 undertaking the same task: the retelling to a therapist of the Cinderella story. The recording lasted about ten minutes for each subject. While clearly such a structured interaction would not provide examples of all the pragmatic features listed in the two profiles, it was felt that this was outweighed by the direct comparability of the two recordings.

4.1.2 *Assessors*
For the purpose of this initial study, the assessments were undertaken by two assessors. Both were lecturers in Higher Education: assessor one being a speech pathologist with a particular interest in pragmatics, assessor two a linguistics lecturer concentrating on pragmatics but with little knowledge of clinical linguistics. It was hoped that this difference in background might well prove a good test of inter-scorer reliability; in further work on this study it would clearly be important to test this reliability with a larger population of assessors.

4.1.3 *Assessments*
The assessors viewed the video as often as they wished while completing the forms. It was felt that this mirrored clinical practice where videos of patients would be utilised: live completion of the profiles being clearly more difficult. They were asked to comment on the time it took to undertake the task and the relative ease or difficulty, and the clinician assessor was asked for his comments on its usefulness in planning remediation. Both scorers commented that the two-point scale of the Pragmatic Protocol was too restrictive, and also that the term 'appropriate' could be misleading as they were unsure as to whether they should

judge in terms of normal speakers, or in terms of the actual communicative event they had watched.

4.2 Results

4.2.1 Inter-scorer reliability
Inter-scorer reliability has been calculated in terms of percentage agreement of classifications. Tables showing these are described below.

As can be seen in Table 1, with the Pragmatic Protocol, the overall percentage agreement was 70%, with agreement on Mr D. at 73.3%, and on Mrs T. at 66.6%. Generally speaking the sections where the two assessors disagreed most were common to both patients.

Table 1. *Interscorer Reliability: Pragmatic Protocol*

	Agreements	Disagreements	Percent Agreement
Mr D	22	8	73.3%
Mrs T	20	10	66.6%
Overall	42	18	70.0%

As is seen in Table 2, the sections with the lowest agreement levels were A (Speech Acts), and F (Paralinguistic aspects). Agreement in section B (Topic) was low for Mrs T. Disagreements were fairly evenly distributed between the three categories of appropriate/inappropriate/no opportunity to observe.

Table 2. *Sectional Interscorer Reliability: Pragmatic Protocol*

	Agreements	Disagreements	Percent Agreement
A	2	2	50%
B	5	3	63%
C	18	0	100%
D	3	1	75%
E	2	0	100%
F	2	8	20%
G	10	4	71%

Tables 3 and 4 show inter-scorer reliability percentages for the PCA. These show an overall rate of 31.1%, with Mr D. at 35.5% and Mrs T. at 26.6%. Figures were also calculated for agreement in terms of broader categories so that they could be directly comparable to the Protocol. These were 'appropriate' (taking in

Penn's III, IV, and V), 'inappropriate' (combining Penn's I, II) and 'no opportunity to observe' (VI). Table 4 shows that worked out in this way we have an overall agreement percentage of 64.4%, with Mr D. at 60% and Mrs T. at 64.4%.

Table 3. *Interscorer Reliability: PCA*

	Agreements	Disagreements	Percent Agreement
Mr D	16	29	35.5%
Mrs T	12	33	26.6%
Overall	28	62	31.1%

Table 5 has also been worked out on the three broader categories noted above, and shows that most disagreement was found in Section 1 (Response to Interlocutor), and in Section 3 (Cohesion). There were no major differences between section scores for the two patients, and again disagreements were fairly evenly distributed between the categories.

Table 4. *Interscorer Reliability: PCA, Broad categories*

	Agreements	Disagreements	Percent Agreement
Mr D	27	18	60.0%
Mrs T	31	14	68.8%
Overall	58	32	64.4%

Table 5: *Sectional Interscorer Reliability: PCA*

	Agreements	Disagreements	Percent Agreement
1	5	5	50%
2	9	3	75%
3	8	6	57%
4	12	2	86%
5	11	7	61%
6	13	9	59%

It is interesting to note that the sections with high disagreements were not identical between the two procedures. Also the very low agreement on the PCA suggests that these two procedures present differing requirements to the assessor. We want to turn now to the main difference between them: the scoring scales.

4.2.2 *Scoring sensitivity comparison*

We have seen from the data above that the five point scale of the PCA dramatically decreases inter-scorer reliability. However, the assessors themselves both commented on their preference for the five point scale over the two point scale.

Apart from the data shown in Tables 3 and 4, we can also look at the information each procedure gives us regarding overall appropriateness. The Protocol allows us to compare simply overall numbers of appropriate and inappropriate parameters (as well as, of course, how useful the session was in providing measurable parameters). The PCA allows us a more sensitive set of figures, perhaps enabling a therapist to review a patient's progress in the redevelopment of pragmatic skills over time.

Total numbers of each category can naturally be worked out for the various sections of our two procedures, but in Table 6 we show only overall figures. These data are derived from the clinician assessor only. It must be remembered that the two procedures are not assessing exactly the same behaviours, nevertheless we do see that the results in this table are considerably different in terms of overall classification of the patients. Whereas the Protocol claims that, as we might expect from the case notes, Mr D. used inappropriate pragmatic behaviours at a level of 33%, and Mrs T. only at a level of 17%; the PCA figures for categories I and II total 16% and 14% respectively. Even if we allowed for category III to be counted in with these, the difference would not be large.

Table 6.   *Category Scores: Assessor 1*

Protocol	Inappropriate	Appropriate	Not Observe
Mr D	10 (33.3%)	15 (50%)	5 (17%)
Mrs T	5 (17%)	23 (76%)	2 (7%)

PCA	I	II	%	III	IV	V	%	VI	%
Mr D	3	4	16%	4	5	21	67%	8	17%
Mrs T	4	2	14%	2	2	24	62%	11	24%

It is well known, of course, that two-point scales force a decision on an assessor, whereas five-point scales often lead to an over-use of the intermediate or neutral category, minimising the likelihood of clear differences emerging. In this case, in fact, assessor one made great use of the fully appropriate category on the PCA rather than the neutral, although assessor two did use this latter quite frequently. While we are not claiming that a two-point scale is always superior to a five point one, it may well be that an area such as pragmatics is better served by a simpler scoring system as a way of minimising the effects of subjective assessing discussed earlier.

At this stage in our investigation it is, perhaps, too early to reach conclusions on the relative merits of the two scoring systems, but it would appear that what assessors want in a profile may not always produce results that tie in with other observations of the patients concerned.

4.2.3 *Diagnostic aspects*
We would like very briefly to comment on the diagnostic aspects of the profiles, again using the clinician assessor's results. We might expect from the previous assessments, and the types of aphasia involved, to see Mr D. performing worse on any profile of pragmatics than Mrs T., albeit long periods of therapy should mean that worse might not mean totally inappropriate behaviour.

Indeed, the Protocol backs up this view, in that Mrs T. has higher scores of appropriateness than Mr D., and lower scores of inappropriateness. However, the PCA has Mr D. with a slightly better set of scores for the three appropriate categories, although the main appropriate category (V) does show that slight difference reversed. In the inappropriate categories Mr D. is only very slightly higher than Mrs T.

It would seem, then, that the enhanced sensitivity of scoring on the PCA has not, in this instance, produced a clearer result for diagnosis purposes. Naturally, the scores of further assessors need to be examined before a firmer conclusion can be reached. We would also wish to compare the results with patterns suggested by Prutting and Kirchner for the Protocol and by Penn for the PCA as typical of different aphasic groups. An initial brief look suggests some similarity (but by no means total) between assessor one's results on the Protocol and patterns described in Prutting and Kirchner (1987).

5. Discussion

The study described above demonstrates the potential problems of assessing pragmatic behaviour. However, we do not want to give the impression that approaches such as the profiles noted above are without merit. The chief obstacles to consistent scorer responses on the profiles appeared to be agreement on what constituted appropriate vs. inappropriate behaviour, and the problem thrown up by using multiple degrees of appropriateness. It is of course quite possible to overcome these problems (at least to some extent) through training of scorers, and perhaps also restriction of scoring choices on any revised version of a profile.

In order to examine some of these difficulties and how one might overcome them in more detail, we will look at an extract of discourse between an aphasic speaker and non-aphasic conversational partners. The following example is a transcript of a conversation involving a patient (P), her husband (H), her son (S), and daughter (D) and a student therapist (T)

1.   T: and write it down
2.   P: yes yes and er er er er er about half past (.) twelve (.) you get
          er your (*demonstrates exercises*) er er er oh dear (1.0)
3   H: exercises
4   D: dad
5   P: exe (*waves hands*) (*all laugh*) ex (*all laugh*)
6   H: I know what she's trying to say you see (*laughter*)
7   P: exercises (*demonstrates exercises*) that's like this (.) you know
          (*waves hand*) and er about five (.) after that it be dinner time
          (2.0) then we get our dinner (1.0) and then come back and then
          (3 syll) they that they play um er (7.0; *writes 'S' in the air;*
          continues to make a waving gesture; 8.0) er (4.0) er er to do
          with er ah er scribble ah scrabble scrabble
8   S: scrabble
9.   T: uhuh
10   P: yes

(Lesser and Milroy, 1993: 214)

This transcript demonstrates repair strategies undertaken by P faced with instances of word-finding difficulty. We can now consider how, using profiles of the type explored above, we might assess this conversation for pragmatic appropriateness.

We might first examine the opening exchange between T and P (turn 1–2). P clearly demonstrates features listed under 'fluency' on the PCA chart: repetitions ("yes yes"); pauses, both filled ("er er er er") and unfilled ((1.0)); word-finding difficulties (presumably noted by "oh dear" as well as the pauses); and incomplete phrases (in that turn 2 ends with the main word-finding difficulty). There are also some features of the non-verbal communication category in turn 2, when P uses gestures to demonstrate the concept of 'exercise', which is, of course, the word she is looking for.

It is clear that the fluency features would be inappropriate in a normal speaker, although they are not all of the same severity. For example, a repetition such as P's "yes yes" is encountered often enough in normal speech, whereas the four filled pauses following ("er er er er") would not be. However, we must remember that the profiles we looked at earlier seem to suggest that judgements of appropriate vs. inappropriate need to be made in terms of the context of the disordered speaker and the particular conversational set-up. It could well be argued, therefore, that when suffering from word-finding problems, the four-fold repetition of the filled pause is appropriate, as it (i) signals that there is a word-finding difficulty, and (ii) signals that the speaker is not willing to yield the floor to other interlocutors but intends to carry on searching for the word required. On the other hand, the unfilled pauses (especially the long pauses of a second or more) might be considered inappropriate, as they do not signal an intention to keep the floor, and indeed the pause at the end of turn 2 leads directly to an interruption at turn 3 by H, who supplies the wanted word.

Turning to the other points raised in this turn, we can see that in this context the non-verbal behaviour was effective, in that H is able to deduce the word wanted (although, as H claims, he may have known the word from the context anyway). Without video evidence to check on the nature of the gestures used, we presumably have to mark this part of the turn as appropriate.

The word-finding difficulties that are evident throughout the extract are clearly greater than those found in normal disfluencies. However, considering the PCA categories, it is difficult to work out how a feature such as this can be classed as 'some appropriate' or 'mostly inappropriate'. It should perhaps be made clear that the terms can also be glossed as 'a few more than normal speakers would use', 'quite a lot more than normal speakers would use' and so on.

In turn 7, which is P's other long turn, a few more features occur as well as the ones we saw in turn 2. There is at least one false start ("and then come back and then (3 syll) they that they play um er"), with an earlier part of the turn also possibly of that category ("and er about five (.) after that it be dinner time"). While false starts are often encountered in normal speech, these examples are complicated by syntactic oddities ("it be dinnertime"), repetitions ("they that they play") and filled and unfilled pauses. This demonstrates another difficulty with assessing pragmatic behaviours: disentangling multiple aspects. Of course, the profiles noted above list pragmatic behaviours separately: this is good discipline for the assessor to ensure all aspects are looked for. However, in real life, many of these aspects interact making it difficult to know how to score any one of them. It could be argued, for example, that the occurrence of a couple of false starts is not in itself inappropriate, however the repetitions and pauses (as we saw earlier) are atypical with this speaker. Does that mean that the false starts should also be classed as inappropriate? The directions to completing pragmatic profiles are normally unclear on such questions.

Finally, in turn 7, we have further examples of the use of gesture. Unlike in turn 2, it would appear that the gestures used when trying to find the word "scrabble" are more extensive. On one hand, the drawing of 'S' in the air might be thought of as an appropriate attempt to get round the problem faced by P; on the other the fact that the gestures continue for so long is clearly inappropriate in terms of normal speech, and probably also in terms of this conversation, as P has to supply the word eventually and the gesture is not interpretable by the audience.

Apart from what we have discussed in relation to this extract, further questions remain to be asked. Chief among them is the relative weighting of the parameters used in the profiles. If someone scores badly on fluency, is this more or less important than a good score on turn-taking? How useful are the sections on these charts — and should they too have a relative weighting. Are they relatable to remediation procedures, or simply constructs of the linguist? On a more practical level, should the charts provide more room for comments and examples, and so perhaps be spread over several pages in a way so that links between sections can be made explicit?

As noted earlier, even if we resolve some of these more mechanical problems, we also need to see clear directions or course material to train assessors in the use of specific pragmatic profiles. With developments in multi-media and distance learning it is surely going to become more straightforward to provide convincing examples of a range of pragmatic disorders, and demonstrations of how the transcribed samples should be entered onto profile charts. At that point we might be able to see more clearly how such charts inform both our diagnosis and treatment.

6. Conclusion

This initial account has demonstrated some of the problems involved in profiling areas of communication that are less concrete than many of the traditional concerns of clinical linguistics. It is clear from the data presented, that clinician training in pragmatic analysis is essential to avoid the discrepancies in inter-scorer reliability that we have seen. If everyone is recording the same behaviour in the same way, then a pragmatic profile is of worth, otherwise it can only be misleading.

References

Ball, M. J., Davies, E., Duckworth, M. and Middlehurst, R. 1991. "Assessing the assessments: a comparison of two clinical pragmatic profiles". *Journal of Communication Disorders* 24: 367–79.

Bates, E. 1976. *Language and Context: the Acquisition of Pragmatics.* New York: Academic Press.

Bedrosian, J. 1985. "An approach to developing conversational competence". In *School Discourse Problems*, D. Ripich and F. Spinelli (eds), London: Taylor and Francis.

Craig, H. 1983. "Applications of pragmatic language models for intervention". In *Pragmatic Assessment and Intervention Issues in Language*, T. Gallagher and C. Prutting (eds). San Diego: College Hill.

Crystal, D., Fletcher, P. and Garman, M. 1976. *The Grammatical Analysis of Language Disability.* London: Edward Arnold.

Davies, G. and Wilcox, M. 1985. *Adult Aphasia Rehabilitation: Applied Pragmatics.* Windsor: NFER-Nelson.

Dewart, H. and Summers, S. 1988. *The Pragmatics Profile of Early Communication Skills.* Windsor: NFER-Nelson.

Gallagher, T. and Prutting, C. (eds) 1983. *Pragmatic Assessment and Intervention Issues in Language.* San Diego: College Hill.

Grundy, P. 1995. *Doing Pragmatics.* London: Edward Arnold.

Grunwell, P. and James, A. (eds) 1989. *The Functional Evaluation of Language Disorders.* London: Croom Helm.

Leech, G. 1983. *Principles of Pragmatics.* London: Longmans.

Lesser, R. and Milroy, L. 1993. *Linguistics and Aphasia.* London: Longmans.

Levinson, S. 1983. *Pragmatics.* Cambridge: Cambridge University Press.

McTear, M. 1985. *Children's Conversations.* Oxford: Blackwell.

McTear, M. and Conti-Ramsden, G. 1989. "Assessment of pragmatics". In *Linguistics in Clinical Practice*, K. Grundy (ed.). London: Taylor and Francis.

Manochiopinig, S., Sheard, C. and Reed, V. 1992. "Pragmatic assessment in adult aphasia: a clinical review". *Aphasiology* 6: 519–533.

Mey, J. 1993. *Pragmatics: an Introduction.* Oxford: Blackwell.

Müller, D., Munro, S. and Code, C. 1981. *Language Assessment for Remediation.* London: Croom Helm.

Penn, C. 1983. *Syntactic and Pragmatic Aspects of Aphasic Language.* Unpublished doctoral thesis, University of the Witwatersrand.

Penn, C. 1988. "The profiling of syntax and pragmatics in aphasia." *Clinical Linguistics & Phonetics* 2: 179–207.

Prutting, C. and Kirchner, D. 1983. "Applied pragmatics". In *Pragmatic Assessment and Intervention Issues in Language*, T. Gallagher and C. Prutting (eds). San Diego: College Hill.

106   MARTIN J. BALL

Prutting, C. and Kirchner, D. 1987. "A clinical appraisal of the pragmatic aspects of language". *Journal of Speech and Hearing Disorders* 52: 105–19.
Roth, F. and Spekman, N. 1984a. "Assessing the pragmatic ability of children: Part 1. Organizational framework and assessment parameters". *Journal of Speech and Hearing Disorders* 49: 2–11.
Roth, F. and Spekman, N. 1984b. "Assessing the pragmatic ability of children: Part 2. Guidelines, considerations, and specific evaluation procedures". *Journal of Speech and Hearing Disorders* 49: 12–17.
Sarno, M. 1969. *The Functional Communication Profile*. New York: New York University Medical Center.
Skinner, C., Wirz, S., Thompson, I. and Davidson, J. 1984. *Edinburgh Functional Communication Profile*. Buckingham: Winslow Press.
Smith, R. 1988. "Pragmatics and speech pathology". In *Theoretical Linguistics and Disordered Language*, M.J. Ball (ed). London: Croom Helm.
Verschueren, J., Östman, J.-O. and Blommaert, J. 1995-. *Handbook of Pragmatics*. Amsterdam: John Benjamins.

Clinical Pragmatics and Assessment of Adult Language Disorders

Process and Product

Claire Penn
University of the Witwatersrand

1. Introduction

A drunk man lost his keys one night, and was observed to be peering at the ground under a street lamp to find them. When asked why he was looking for them there, when he had lost them in the dark bushes some distance away, the drunkard replied, "I know, but it's easier to look for them here."

This anecdote was told to me in 1983 by Carol Prutting in order to illustrate that because some clinical issues are difficult to tackle, the clinician may be dissuaded from seeking relevant routes of understanding a problem and choose instead a standard and well-worn approach to the problem — easy but not necessarily effective. Such, Prutting maintained was the resistance of many clinicians to adopting the paradigm of clinical pragmatics — an observation I believe is as true today as it was then.

A pragmatic approach to the assessment of clinical language problems has been around for nearly twenty years. It is clearly time to take stock and see where this approach has led us, what common beliefs and misconceptions surround the field and to examine critically the adequacy of the plethora of assessment tools that exist. In many ways I suspect that the theoretical and terminological confusions which beleaguered us a long time ago have not been resolved, and that there remain grey areas of overlap which continue to plague those working in the field, particularly the practitioners. What complicates the issue further are the current impinging concepts of impairment, disability and handicap as well as the prominent focus on functional skills which in the framework of adult language pathology also need to be reconciled with the pragmatic approach.

While understanding how and why this focus on functional has come about in terms of the need to be accountable and to measure outcomes effectively in the context of diminishing resources, there is a real fear that this may lead to an oversimplification of issues. We should avoid the danger of examining outcome or effect to the exclusion of understanding the processes which underlie this outcome.

In this chapter I will attempt to reconcile some of these issues and will argue the need for the continuing centrality of a pragmatic paradigm as a framework of both explanation and of relevance in our clinical endeavours.

2.   Defining Pragmatics/Scope

The field of clinical pragmatics has a relatively short history, but is based on a "strong theoretical lineage" which Prutting (1982) in her comprehensive article on the topic carefully traced. The speech act framework of philosophers such as Wittgenstein (1958), Austin (1962) and Searle (1969) and later of linguists such as Bates (1976) and Levinson (1983), informed the essence of the pragmatic debate in the early eighties. Among central issues of discussion were: whether pragmatics could be considered as separate from structural aspects of language, or whether pragmatics was part of a continuum with linguistics; the precise role of speech act theory in the realm of pragmatics; the definition of context, some preferring to define it in linguistic terms only, others incorporating extralinguistic and social context aspects as well.

In 1987, Prutting and Kirchner wrote that there was no single agreed-upon paradigm of pragmatics and that researchers were still in a period of fact-gathering in order to determine what the pragmatic aspects of language are and how these should be organised for clinical and research purposes. Despite this apparent lack of a uniform paradigm, certain cornerstones to the field could undoubtedly be identified. These were:

2.1   *The Acknowledgement of a Synergistic Perspective of Language Behaviour*

This was discussed in an infrequently cited but very powerful example of writing by Prutting and Elliott (1979):

> Scientists have primarily examined component parts of a system independently, placing minor emphasis on the phenomena as they exist and operate within a

total system. It can be argued that the measurements of component parts reflect in a quantified manner some descriptive aspect of artificially or externally defined or segmented phenomena. However these measurements do not necessarily reflect how the component parts relate to one another in a system or how the total system operates.

The merging of linguistic, cognitive and social aspects within the domain of pragmatics enabled a holistic synergistic view of the whole process of language (Bates 1976). Thus in contrast to previous modular unidimensional, taxonomic perspectives of language, pragmatic theorists focused on the interacting relationship between units of languages.

2.2 The Importance of Multidimensional Pragmatic Assessment and Profiling

Following from this synergistic perspective of language, the importance of a multidimensional framework of language assessment emerged. Detailed profiling of language behaviour incorporated a consideration of descriptions in other domains such as cognitive and social ones. Within this framework the opportunity for an inter-explanatory framework emerged. In different clinical cases, writers sought for parallels and dissociations in communicative cognitive and social domains (McTear 1985). The focus of concern became language beyond the sentence level, that is at the level of connected discourse and assessment in differing contexts was seen as an integral component of adequate diagnosis.

2.3 The Importance of a Theory-driven Approach to Clinical Endeavour

The pragmatic framework aimed to seek explanation for clinical behaviours observed. It was viewed as an alternative theoretical paradigm to explain the complexities of communication and one which provided strong competition to generative theories of language (Prutting 1983; Gallagher 1991).

It was argued that a theory-driven approach would lead directly to assessment and therapy planning, and provide the clinician with an alternative and individualised method of describing and explaining clinical behaviour. Social validation was seen as a central construct in goal of assessment and therapeutic endeavour. The focus of concern is not only on what language the person has, but also the intentions behind it, how language is used and what effect such behaviours had on social relationships. While many early studies conducted under the umbrella of clinical pragmatics adhered to some or all of the above pragmatic principles, it would appear that as the complexity of the domain emerged, individual studies examined increasingly splintered components of the larger field.

Another trend was the emergence of taxonomy-based descriptions yielding scores rather than composite profiles, and often insufficiently linked to the original and underlying theory. Some dissatisfaction emerged concerning the psychometric properties of available measures (Ball *et al.* 1991; cf. also Ball, this volume) as well as disagreement regarding the terms of reference.

Thus in much of the so-called applied pragmatics research conducted within the clinical framework, it appeared that the underlying theoretical cornerstones became neglected or in some cases forgotten in a search for clinical accountability and relevance.

3.   Impairment, Disability and Handicap

The World Health Organisation framework of impairment, disability and handicap (1980) was developed as a unifying conceptual scheme for understanding the nature of injury and its sequelae in the life of the individual. Originally expounded in detail in professions other than speech-language pathology, the classification was adapted in our field as reflected in the recent publications which highlight the difference in relation to the communication sphere (Frattali *et al.* 1995; Raaijmakers *et al.* 1995). In her comprehensive review of this framework Worrall (1992, 1995) defines the concepts as follows:

> *Impairment*: any loss or abnormality of psychological, physiological or anatomical structure or functions.
> *Disability*: Any restriction or lack resulting from an impairment of ability to perform an activity in the manner or within the range considered normal for a human being.
> *Handicap*: the disadvantage that limits or prevents fulfilment of a role that is normal, depending on age, sex or socio-cultural factors. This thus includes issues such as physical independence and mobility, roles and activities, social integration and economic self sufficiency.

The differentiation between these three aspects has become the underpinning for differentiated assessment in a number of speech and language disorders including aphasia and closed head injury. (See e.g. Hartley 1995; Heinemann and Whiteneck 1995). For example in aphasia, the anatomical basis for *impairment* is well established. Its sequelae are also well documented (e.g. aphasia types etc.) including the psychological sequelae (as measured on depression scales for example). Assessment of impairment includes a range of neurological examinations; traditional standard batteries of speech/language and of personality factors yield a score or profile of the impairment.[1]

The notion of *disability* with regard to communication disorders reflects the consequences of the impairment in terms of everyday performance for the individual (Worrall 1995). These are disturbances at the personal level for the individual and thus include abilities such as answering the telephone, take messages, count change and the use of social conventions (Frattali *et al.* 1995).

Handicap is concerned with the value society and the individual attaches to the particular skill. The disadvantages to the individual in the wider social context as a result of impairment and disability thus are considered. This reflects as Enderby (1992) points out "interaction with and adaptation to, the individual's surroundings... handicap can only be classified according to the circumstances in which disabled people are likely to find themselves in a relation to peers and society, and not according to the individual's attributes alone". Communication difficulties can handicap an individual vocationally, socially and recreationally. The context of the individual thus becomes paramount and assessment tools require the central construct of social validation as evaluation of handicap takes place in family and work settings (see for example Campbell and Dollaghan 1992). Hence the opinions of significant others such as spouses and employers become important in delineating the extent or the effect of handicap of the individual. A good example of such a scale is the Communicative Effectiveness Index (CETI) devised by Lomas *et al.* (1989) in which the significant others of aphasic patients are required to rate their performance on sixteen everyday items relative to their performance before the stroke.

There is a hypothesised linear relationship between these three constructs which has been demonstrated in some disorders but does not always seem to fit when we examine some adult language disorders and their most common forms of assessment (Heinemann and Whiteneck 1995; Frattali 1992; Enderby 1992). It has become obvious that there are not necessarily linear or causal relationships in all populations. For example, the aphasic individual may demonstrate significant impairments at the level of discrete traditional testing, and yet may exhibit intact functional skills as measured on a scale of functional communicative efficiency. Conversely, a traumatically brain injured individual often presents little or no deficit on formal traditional tests, that is, no impairment, but substantial functional problems both in the everyday and wider social contexts, that is at the level of disability and handicap (Hartley 1995). In these populations, cognitive factors became as important in explaining the profile of disability and handicap as linguistic features and should rightly receive equal if not more attention in both assessment and therapy. The need for multidimensional profiling such as that implicit in a pragmatic approach thus emerges.

4. Pragmatic Assessment

What is meant by pragmatic assessment and how is this differentiated from other types of communication assessment? There have been numerous and comprehensive reviews of the field of pragmatic assessment in recent years, most of which discuss the procedures and aims of each test. Until recently, few have tried to group or describe tests according to their theoretical bases and when they do, different groupings emerge (Manochiopinig *et al.* 1992; Hough and Pierce 1994). This appears to be due to confusion as to which tests are in actual fact pragmatic assessments and which are functional tests (or both). If we are to maintain clarity in the conceptual bases of testing and terminology, it seems worth the effort to distinguish between the pragmatic and functional measures.

It would seem that many of the tests reviewed as pragmatic assessments are in actual fact outcome measures and should be classified as functional tests, even though some may indirectly measure some aspects of pragmatic behaviour, e.g. the Communicative Abilities in Daily Living (CADL) (Holland 1983), or may be based on pragmatic principles, e.g. Sarno's Functional Communication Profile (1969). Some functional tests have been classified as being tests of disability (Frattali *et al.* 1995), while those that include the social and vocational domains or require the rating of communicative efficiency by significant others, tap the handicap aspect as well.

Table 1 provides a sample of some of the more frequently cited assessment tools and attempts to separate some of the many tools that exist according to pragmatic versus functional dimensions. It further distinguishes those functional tests which tend to tap disability-related aspects from those which measure handicap (see also Ferguson (this volume) who comments on assessment tools valid for identification of communication strategies).

The pragmatic measures have in common, their basis in a theoretical framework (such as speech act theory) and a multidimensional perspective of both linguistic and non-linguistic elements. These include the Pragmatic Protocol (Prutting and Kirchner 1987), the Profile of Communicative Appropriateness (PCA) (Penn 1985), the Assessment Protocol of Pragmatic-Linguistic Skills (APPLS) (Gerber and Gurland 1989) and the Edinburgh Functional Communication profile and its revised version (Skinner *et al.* 1984; Wirz *et al.* 1990).

Functional assessment measures by contrast are those which reflect the combined effectiveness of a number of pragmatic (including linguistic/cognitive/ social) behaviours in achieving functional communication. The component pragmatic behaviours are *not* directly identified and the explanations for these are not sought. Rather it is the end measure (or end product) of a person's ability to function in real-life situations that is the goal of functional assessment (Manochiopinig *et al.* 1992). The most recently worked out example is the American Speech-Language Hearing Association Functional Assessment of Communication Skills for Adults (ASHA FACS). This is a "generalist" measure for assessing functional communication which the authors propose addresses the WHO classification scheme at the level of disability measurement, and not impairment or handicap, and is hence designed to complement measures of these two aspects. The domains of assessment represent a shift from the traditional categories of verbal expression, speech intelligibility and auditory comprehension to the following four areas: social communication, communication of basic needs, daily planning, and reading, writing and number concepts (Frattali *et al.* 1995).

The ASHA FACS is a most timely assessment tool that has come about at a time of much discussion of functional assessment theory and practice (see for example *Aphasiology* 1992). Elman and Bernstein-Ellis (1995) in fact suggest that "It has become almost impossible to write a treatment plan or submit a claim to a third party payer without using the word *functional*. A speech-language pathologist must identify functional goals, use functional tasks and show functional gains, or reimbursement for treatment is likely to be denied".

It appears that the FACS has addressed a number of the methodological complaints that have dogged most of the tools to date. Pilot data reveals adequate psychometric properties of inter-rater reliability (mean correlation of .90), intra-rater reliability (mean correlation of .99), external validity (moderately high correlations with other measures of language and cognition) and internal validity. It appears to distinguish between different severity levels as well as between clinical populations e.g. stroke and closed head injury. The authors openly acknowledge that the FACS is not detailed enough for specialised assessment of clinical populations and does not measure the functional consequences of aphasia. It is purely an outcome measure which may have more value for policy makers than to therapists. In fact, Elman and Bernstein-Ellis (1995) argue that even the term functional which appears to represent a shared frame of reference for different professions has different definitions and scope in relation to certain populations.

The significant overlap between terms and assessment domains under the umbrella of 'functional', particularly between the categories of disability and

Table 1.   *Classification of communication assessment tools.*

Test Type	Tests
Pragmatic Assessment	Pragmatic Protocol (Prutting and Kirchner 1983) Profile of Communicative Appropriateness (PCA) (Penn 1988) Assessment of Pragmatic-Linguistic Skills (APPLS) (Gerber and Gurland 1989) Sections of the Discourse Abilities Profile (DAP) (Terrel and Ripich 1989) Edinburgh Functional Communication Profile (EFCP) (Skinner *et al.* 1984) Revised Edinburgh Functional Communication Profile (R-EFCP) (Wirz *et al.* 1990)
Functional Assessment (Disability)	Functional Communication Profile (FCP) (Sarno 1969) Communicative Abilities of Daily Living (CADL) (Holland 1980) The Rating of Functional Performance (Wertz *et al.* 1981) The Communicative Competence Evaluation Instrument (CCEI) (Houghton *et al.* 1982) The Amsterdam-Nijmegen Everyday Language Test (ANELT) (Blomert 1990) The Everyday Communication Needs Assessment (ECNA) (Worrall 1995) The Functional Linguistic Communication Inventory (FLCI) (Bayles and Tomeoda 1995) Functional Assessment of Communication Skills for Adults (ASHA FACS) (Frattali *et al.* 1995)
Functional Assessment (Handicap/ social validation)	A questionnaire rating personal/communicative style (Swindell *et al.* 1982) The Communicative Effectiveness Index (CETI) (Lomas *et al.* 1989) Checklist of Adaptive Listening Skills (CALS) (Morreau and Bruininks 1991) Adult Social Communication Rating Scale (Hough, in Hough and Pierce 1989

handicap commented on by Worrall (1992) indicates it might be that while the WHO framework of description is a useful one for other behavioural domains (such as physical disability), it may be too limiting in considering the complexities of communication behaviour.

In a close examination of all the above measures two paradoxes emerge. The first relates to the psychometric properties of these scales, an aspect discussed by Ball *et al.* (1991) (cf. also Ball, this volume) as well as by Mano-chiopinig *et al.* (1992). A point of note is that some of the scales used frequently, especially those with a functional basis, appear to have robust psychometric validity because of their relative ease of administration. It is probably true to say that the more functional a measure becomes, the easier it is to administer and the higher therefore measures such as reliability, no doubt because these scales are measuring highly observable end-product skills. While Frattali (1992) points out the irony that decisions in health care policy are often based on tools of questionable reliability and validity, an equally unacceptable scenario is that outcome measures become so psychometrically refined and simplistic that they fail to reflect the complex process factors associated with outcome (cf. Enderby 1992). Further, outcome measures should not be confused with the diagnostic purposes of assessment. If a measure is treatment-driven, it should be multidimensional and address both symptoms and their interrelationships in order to understand how best they can be modified. It should also differentiate between populations whose essential underlying deficit is different. Once again, regrettably the easiest measures tend to provide the fewest directions for therapy. The tools which perhaps present with the most difficulty and require the most experience are those that yield potentially the most clinical information. There is a very real fear that taxonomic functional evaluation can become almost mechanistic in administration, a warning knell to language clinicians who strive for continued professional autonomy. In other words it can happen that assessment which focuses too much on measurable skills deprives the clinician of insights necessary for effective treatment.

A further concern is the cross-cultural application of some of these measures. As authors such as Argyle (1975) have pointed out, many different cultural constraints operate in interpersonal situations. The use of social conventions differs among communities. In South Africa for example, lack of eye contact is seen as courteous in certain conversational contexts; turn initiation and requests for clarification or elaboration are also sometimes interpreted as being disrespectful; there are differences in terms of body proxemics etc. with different interlocutors.

Chick (1990a: 235) writes that there is anecdotal evidence that Zulu English speakers speak more slowly than white English speakers, that pauses of relatively short duration do not function as turn-exchange signals in Zulu English and that Zulu English speakers are generally more tolerant of extended dialogue than white English speakers. In his own study, he found that different pragmatic behaviours such as deference and potential loss of face in an interaction gave rise to asynchrony in inter-cultural dyads and lead to "misinterpretation, mis-evaluation, prejudice and reinforcement of a negative cycle of socially created discrimination" (1990a: 254). Other South African inter-cultural studies clearly highlight such difficulties which arise in situations such as the law court (Kaschula 1995) and in local governmnet settings (Fordred 1995). Given such cultural differences, some of the items of the FACS may thus for example be inappropriate for the South African context, e.g. begins conversations with other people; requests that conversational partner repeat, clarify or slow down when necessary.

Further the FACS, as well as many of the functional (and traditional) scales places a high premium on literacy, which becomes an issue of little or no functional relevance in the assessment of an illiterate patient with no education, e. g. follows written directions; understands simple reading material; follows a map; makes a short list; writes messages. A cursory examination reveals that for the above reasons, at least one third of the ASHA FACS items, for example, would not be entirely suitable for measuring disability in a significant proportion of South African patients.

At the handicap level, cross-cultural differences also emerge. In a study undertaken with the significant others of aphasic and right hemisphere patients across four different cultural and linguistic groups in South Africa, some interesting functional differences appeared to emerge (Penn, Milner and Fridjhon 1992). While quantitatively their communicative deficit seemed to be compara-ble, qualitatively, the items judged to be handicapping were different across the cultural groups. For example the item participating in a conversation with strangers was found to be very difficult to white English- and Afrikaans-speaking patients, whereas to Zulu- and Sotho-speaking patients, this situation seemed to pose fewer functional difficulties. Conversely, black patients were judged to show greater difficulty indicating understanding of what was being said than white patients. These findings were hypothesised to be a function of different cultural norms and attitudes towards disability. Contextual factors thus assume major significance in a consideration of functional relevance.

In addition, in assessment of handicap, one must consider the fact that many patients function in several cultural spheres as part of their daily lives e.g. work and home. This highlights the importance of Ferguson's point (this volume) that assessment in different settings enhances validity of sampling.

5.   A Model of Explanation and Relevance: Why Not? and So What?

There appears to be a need to reconcile the notions that have been discussed and to consider their relationship to clinical practice. Our two main clinical responsibilities are to seek explanation for what we find, and to account for what we do. It is simply irresponsible to ignore either of these aspects. I believe that pragmatic assessment provides a useful framework for both explanation and relevance. This is further exemplified by the model in Figure 1 which attempts to reflect the centrality of pragmatic assessment in relation to the issues raised in the above discussion both in relation to the term 'functional' and within the frame of reference of the WHO classification scheme.

Examples of measurement tools for each of the categories are illustrated as well as the questions which should guide the assessment in each of the areas. Thus for instance, the measure of impairment is measured by a range of standardised tests suitable for the particular level of breakdown while a rating scale such as the CETI would be used to measure handicap.

Taking functional disability as the central perspective, best exemplified by FACS, I would suggest that, having determined functional impairment in an individual, two major questions should be asked: *why not?* and *so what?* The question "Why not?" leads to the delineation of the impairment and thus provides the basis of an *explanation* for the functional difficulty. The question "So what?" leads to the delineation of the level of handicap and thus explores the *relevance* namely the effect or the socially significant aspects of the disability. Both of these are the key components of a pragmatic approach.

In focusing on the "why not" and the "so what", pragmatics through multidimensional profiling incorporates cognitive, linguistic and non-linguistic factors (impairment) as well as social and cultural factors (disability and handicap). Some of the underlying behaviours that incorporate such aspects can be found in an examination of syntax, phonology (linguistic), memory (cognitive), conversation, turn taking, facial expression, posture (non verbal behaviour) to name but a few. By profiling simultaneously such 'discrete' or molecular *pragmatic* skills we hope to explain the disability observed in functional testing.

In fact, as can be seen in the model, pragmatic competence can be measured at each of the levels of impairment, disability and handicap and it may be in the examination of the relationship between these abilities that the nature of the relationship between the three classifications may emerge.

Unless the issues of explanation and relevance are addressed, I do not believe that we can really be effective in therapy. To delineate the functional skills the patients has, is not the same as being able to identify what is required

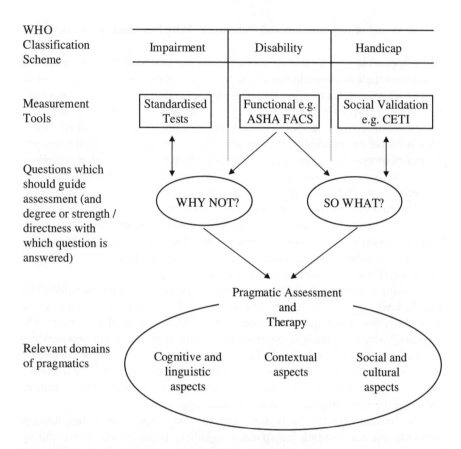

Figure 1.   *A Synergistic Model of Explanation and Relevance*

in order to modify his/her level of handicap. Merely to state that a person cannot
communicate with a stranger on a telephone, gets us no nearer to being able to
describe the factors which contribute to that and whether this is a relevant skill
for that person. Equally to say that the person has dysarthria brings us no closer
to being able to describe what the effect of this will be in functional terms.
Pragmatic assessment explores both structural and functional features simultaneously while examining the patient in context in order to describe and explain
when and why he performs functionally and how, when and why he does not. In
other words, we need to know what factor or cluster of factors makes a difference to producing a functional communicator.

A functional assessment by contrast tends to document the observable effects, that is, what you see. Taken to the extreme, what you see is all you will have to work on in therapy. A functional test may in fact not be assessing the direct result of discrete impairments only but the interaction between such impairments and the intact (or otherwise) other pragmatic abilities of the patient that go undetected on standard tests.

Worrall (1995) points out that a functional communication approach can easily be misconstrued as a "non theoretical, common sense approach to the treatment to aphasia". While acknowledging Worrall's attempt to systematise the notion of functional within the WHO framework, we should heed Hempel's (1966: 71) reminder that "a conceptual system that conveys insight into the phenomenon in (an) intuitive sense does not for that reason alone qualify as a scientific theory". Scientific theory seeks to explain uniformities in a class of phenomena and the entities and processes that lie behind and beneath them. The WHO framework, while potentially providing a fruitful division for consideration as Worrall asserts, by its nature cannot be as productive as a pragmatic basis for providing explanation. A more holistic and balanced perspective potentially allows the therapist to be accountable in the true sense. While President of ASHA, Logemann, in 1993, cautioned: "Clinicians always need to be able to answer the question 'Why are you doing what you are doing?' If they are not able to do so, they will not last long in what they are doing". Pragmatic assessment *by definition* serves potentially to integrate the artificial gap between the handicap, impairment and disability sides of the scale.

The strong correlation between functional and standard tests commented on by writers such as Wertz (1995: 313) is no small coincidence — they ultimately reflect two sides of the one pragmatic coin. A synergistic pragmatic approach might be more productive than to attempt to create artificial categories for considering communicative breakdown. Scheffler (1967) has in fact pointed out that categorical systems cannot be viewed as objective instruments of science and cannot be tested for truth value. Our vision/perspective may become limited by traditional categories and by assessment measures which are too narrowly focused. The danger is that in trying to be too modular, one loses the intricate relationship between structure and function that is the linguistic-pragmatic relationship. These are the complex synergistic interrelated processes through which meaningful explanation and clinical practice are derived.

A pragmatic approach potentially provides a theoretical framework which according to Volpe (1981) takes the clinician beyond the role of practical wisdom to that of "scientist-scholar", who thus has access to a "breadth of perspective unobtainable in a lifetime of experience".

6. Conclusion

The current focus on functional and what may be perceived as the confounding complexity of pragmatics should not in any way deter us from continued attempts to seek synergistic and detailed explanations of what we observe and what we attempt to treat. The answers may not be simple but they are worth searching for.

A functional communication approach to aphasia seems to have become confused with a pragmatic approach and I believe should be considered as clearly distinct. In effect, a pragmatic approach to aphasia necessarily embraces functional considerations, but provides the clinician with a broader and theoretically driven framework for assessment and intervention, the *sine qua non* of progress in the scientific status of our relatively new profession, and ultimately its long term repute (cf. Prutting 1983).

The current ethos of accountability and relevance leads us quite legitimately to strive for examination of outcome. Nevertheless it should be borne in mind that however much pressure received from funding agents, outcome should be *one* goal but not the only goal of therapy. As Enderby (1992) points out, an outcome to a patient may not necessarily be measured only in terms of the scales that we apply; the process should not be forgotten. A failure to integrate assessment within a framework of both explanation and relevance may lead one to neglect or ignore these central clinical issues. An apt quotation by John Dewey (1934) cited in Strauss and Corbin (1990) illustrates this point effectively: "It is no linguistic accident that 'building', 'construction', [and] 'work' designate both a process and its finished product. Without the meaning of the verb, that of the noun remains blank."

I urge clinicians to remember that process as much as product should be the essence of our clinical concern.

Acknowledgements

This chapter is dedicated to the memory of Carol Prutting whose sudden death in 1989 was a profound loss to the field of applied pragmatics. I met her in 1983 and had the great privilege of working with her, of learning from her and of teaching with her. Sadly our goals of writing together never materialised. Much of what is written here are seeds sown in our joint discussion that have germinated with time and experience. As for many others with whom she worked (see for example the text edited by Gallagher in 1991), her thinking in this area provided me with immeasurable and lasting inspiration. She was a person with rare qualities, not the least of which was an ability to look beyond and through the paradigms of the moment in a search for truth. I have written this chapter in tribute to her — hoping also that through some of these ideas her permanent and lasting impact on the field of pragmatics will continue to live on.

I am deeply indebted to Nola Watt for her considerable assistance in the preparation of this chapter.

Note

1. Disturbingly, some of the current approaches to testing based on cognitive neuropsychology plant us firmly and exclusively back in this domain. Impairments that we never even believed existed, e.g. reading non words, come to the attention of both the patients and the therapist with careful testing, serving the function (in the case of the tester) of proving a modular model of language, but disturbingly also serving the function in the case of the patient of further highlighting his sense of frustration and deficit. Unless such an approach to assessment is followed up (as it should be) by constructive and functional therapy (see Byng (1988) and Lesser and Milroy (1993) for very positive examples of how this can be achieved) it cannot possibly be justified.

References

Argyle, M. 1975. *Bodily Communication*. London: Penguin.

Austin, J. 1962. *How to Do Things With Words*. Cambridge: Harvard University Press.

Ball, M., Davies, E., Duckworth, M. and Middlehurst, R. 1991. "Assessing the Assessments: A comparison of two clinical pragmatic profiles". *Journal of Communication Disorders* 24: 367–379.

Bates, E. M. 1976. *Language in Context*. New York: Academic Press.

Bayles, K. and Tomeoda, C. 1995. *Functional Linguistic Communication Inventory (FLCI)*. Oxon: Winslow Press.

Blomert, L. 1990. "What functional assessment can contribute to setting goals for aphasia therapy". *Aphasiology* 4: 307–320.

Byng, S. 1988. "Sentence processing deficits: theory and therapy". *Cognitive Neuropsychology* 5: 629–676.

Campbell, T. F. and Dollaghan, C. 1992. "A method for obtaining listener judgements of spontaneously produced language: social validation through direct magnitude estimation". *Topics in Language Disorders* 12: 42–55.

Chick, J. K. 1990a. "The interactional accomplishment of discrimination in South Africa". In *Cultural Communication and Inter-Cultural Contact*, D. Carbaugh (ed.), Chapter 16. New Jersey: Lawrence Erlbaum Associates.

Chick, J. K. 1990b. "Reflections on language, interaction and context: micro and macro issues". In *Cultural Communication and Inter-Cultural Contact*, D. Carbaugh (ed.), Chapter 17. New Jersey: Lawrence Erlbaum Associates.

Elman, R. J. and Bernstein-Ellis, E. 1995. "What is functional?". *American Journal of Speech-Language Pathology* 4 (4): 115–117.

Enderby, P. 1992. "Outcome measures in speech therapy: impairment, disability, handicap and distress". *Health Trends* 24 (2): 61–64.

Fordred, L. 1995. "Of communication between comrades and bureaucrats". *People Dynamics* 13: 23–25.

Frattali, C. M. 1992. "Functional assessment of communication: merging public policy with clinical views". *Aphasiology* 6 (1): 63–83.

Frattali, C. M., Thompson, C. M., Holland, A. L., Wohl, C. B., Ferketic, M. M. 1995. "The FACS of life. ASHA FACS — A functional outcome measure for adults". *ASHA* 37 (4): 41–46.

Gallagher, T. M. 1991. *Pragmatics of Language. Clinical Practice Issues*. San Diego: Singular Publishing.

Gerber, S. and Gurland, G. B. 1989. "Applied pragmatics in the assessment of aphasia". *Seminars in Speech and Language* 10 (4): 263–281.

Hartley, L. L. 1995. *Cognitive-Communicative Abilities Following Brain Injury*. San Diego: Singular Publishing.

Heinemann, A. W. and Whiteneck, G. G. 1995. "Relationships among impairment, disability, handicap, and life satisfaction in persons with traumatic brain injury". *Journal of Head Trauma Rehabilitation* 10: 54–63.

Hempel, C. G. 1966. *Philosophy of Natural Science*. Engelwood Cliffs: Prentice Hall.

Holland, A. L. 1980. *Communicative Abilities in Daily Living (CADL): A Test of Functional Communication*. Baltimore: University Park Press.

Hough, M. S. and Pierce, R. S. 1989. "Contextual influence in aphasia: effects of predictive versus non predictive narratives". *Brain and Language* 36: 325–334.

Houghton, P. M., Pettit, J. M., and Towey, M. P. 1982. "Measuring communicative competence in global aphasia". In *Clinical Aphasiology: Conference Proceedings*, R. H. Brookshire (ed.), 28–39. Minneapolis: BRK Publishers.

Kaschula, R. H. 1995. "Cross-cultural communication in the Eastern Cape with particular reference to law courts". *South African Journal of African Languages* 15: 9–15.

Lesser, R. and Milroy, L. 1993. *Linguistics and Aphasia*. London: Longman.

Levinson, S. C. 1983. *Pragmatics*. Cambridge: Cambridge University Press.

Logemann, J. 1993. "Dysphagia and speech-language pathology". Presentation in session entitled: "Speech-language pathology: Moving towards the twenty-first century." ASHA Convention: Anaheim, November 1993.

Lomas, J., Pickard, L., Betser, S., Elbard, H., Finlayson, A. and Zoghaib, C. 1989. "The communicative effectiveness index: development and psychometric evaluation of a functional communication measure for adult aphasia". *Journal of Speech and Hearing Disorders* 54: 113–224.

Manochiopinig, S., Sheard, C. and Reed, V. A. 1992. "Pragmatic assessment in adult aphasia: a clinical review". *Aphasiology* 6 (6): 519–534.

McTear, M. F. 1985. "Pragmatic disorders: a question of direction". *British Journal of Disorders of Communication* 20: 119–127.

Morreau, L. E. and Bruininks, R. H. 1991. *Checklist of Adaptive Listening Skills.* Allen, TX: DLM.

Penn, C. 1988. "The profiling of syntax and pragmatics in aphasia". *Clinical Linguistics and Phonetics* 2: 179–207.

Penn, C., Milner, K. and Fridjhon, P. 1992. "The Communicative Effectiveness Index: its use with South African patients with aphasia and right hemisphere damage". *South African Journal of Communication Disorders* 39: 74–82.

Prutting, C. A. 1982. "Pragmatics as social competence". *Journal of Speech and Hearing Disorders* 47: 123–133.

Prutting C. A. 1983. "Scientific enquiry and communicative disorders: an emerging paradigm across six decades". In *Pragmatic Assessment and Intervention Issues in Language*, T. Gallagher and C. A. Prutting (eds), Chapter 11. San Diego: College Hill Press.

Prutting, C. A. and Elliott, K. B. 1979. "Synergy: toward a model of language". *Speech and Language* 1: 337–365.

Prutting, C. A. and Kirchner, D. 1983. "Applied pragmatics". In *Pragmatic Assessment and Intervention Issues in Language*, T. M. Gallagher and C. A. Prutting (eds), Chapter 2. San Diego: College Hill Press.

Prutting, C. A. and Kirchner, D. 1987. "A clinical appraisal of the pragmatic aspects of language". *Journal of Speech and Hearing Disorders* 52: 105–119.

Raaijmakers, M. F., Dekker, J., Dejonckere, P. H. and van der Zee, J. 1995. "Reliability of the assessment of impairments, disabilities and handicaps in survey research on speech therapy". *Folia Phoniatrica et Logopaedica* 47: 199–209.

Sarno, M. T., 1969 *The Functional Communication Profile.* New York: NYU Medical Centre, Institute of Rehabilitation Medicine.

Scheffler, I. 1967. *Science and Subjectivity.* New York: Howard and Sams.

Searle, J. 1969. *Speech Acts: An Essay in the Philosophy of Language.* Cambridge: Cambridge University Press.

Skinner, C., Wirz, S., Thompson, I. and Davidson, J. 1984. *Edinburgh Functional Communication Profile.* Scotland: Winslow Press.

Strauss, A. and Corbin, J. 1990. *Basics of Qualitative Research.* Newbury Park, California: Sage Publications, Inc.

Swindell, C. S. Pashek, G. V. and Holland, A. L. 1982. "A questionnaire for surveying personal and communicative style". In *Clinical Aphasiology: Conference Proceedings*, R. H. Brookshire (ed.), 50–63. Minneapolis: BRK Publishers.

Terrell, B. Y, and Ripich, D. N. 1989. "Discourse competence as a variable in intervention." *Seminars in Speech and Language* 10: 282–297.

Volpe, R 1981. "Knowledge from theory and practice". *Oxford Review of Education* 7: 41–51.

Wertz, R. T., Collins, M., Weiss, D., Kurtzke, J. F., Friden, T., Brookshire, R. H., Pierce, J., Holzapple, P., Hubbars, D., Porch, B., West, J., Davis, L., Matovich, V., Orley, G. and Resurreccion, E. 1981. "Veterans Administration cooperative study on aphasia: a comparison of individual and group treatment". *Journal of Speech and Hearing Disorders* 24: 580–594.

Wertz, R. T. 1995. "Efficacy". In *Treatment of Aphasia: From Theory to Practice*, C. Code and D. Müller (eds), Chapter 16. London: Whurr

Wittgenstein, L. 1958. *Philosophical Investigations.* New York: MacMillan.

Wirz, S. L., Skinner, C. and Dean, E. 1990. *Revised Edinburgh Functional Communication Profile.* Tucson, AZ: Communication Skill Builders.

World Health Organization, 1980. *International Classification of Impairments, Disabilities and Handicaps.* Geneva: WHO.

Worrall, L. 1992. "Functional communication assessment: an Australian perspective". *Aphasiology* 6 (1): 105–110.

Worrall, L. 1995. "The Functional Communication Perspective". In *Treatment of Aphasia: From Theory to Practice*, C. Code and D. Müller (eds), Chapter 4. London: Whurr.

Applying the Principles of Conversational Analysis in the Assessment and Treatment of a Child with Pragmatic Difficulties

Amanda Willcox
*North Durham Community
Health Care Trust*

Kay Mogford-Bevan
Lostwithiel, Cornwall

1. Introduction

An ever increasing number of children are being identified as having pragmatic difficulties by speech and language therapists, educational psychologists and specialist teachers.

Professionals seem to agree that such children have good formal language skills in that their speech is clearly articulated and grammatically accurate. Such children also seem to achieve age appropriate or above average scores in assessments of the understanding of language. Nevertheless these children find it very difficult to use language to participate in conversation. They seem to be unable to grasp the significance of the context when interpreting what other people say to them, and frequently respond in a way that their conversational partner does not expect. They find it hard to read non-verbal messages like eye-signalling, facial expressions and tone of voice, and as a result often miss the meaning that is actually intended by the speaker. Moreover the manner in which they use language to ask for things, or to comment, is often considered to be rude or unkind. Consequently such children find if difficult to make friends with their peers, and are socially isolated and lonely.

There continues to be considerable debate as to the causes of a communication disorder of this nature, and also as to the most useful diagnostic label. An inability to initiate and to sustain meaningful conversation with others is recognised as one of the criteria in the diagnosis of an autistic disorder (Rutter 1978; Wing 1981, 1988), but it is evident that not all children who present with difficulties in conversation are autistic. Similarly, many children who present with grammatical or phonological disorders also have difficulties participating in conversation (Gallagher and Darnton 1978; Donahue, Pearl and Bryan 1980; Brinton and Fujiki 1982; Conti-Ramsden and Friel-Patti 1983; Fey and Leonard 1983; Craig and Evans 1989). However, there is no evidence to suggest that all those children with a pragmatic impairment have a history of delayed or disordered grammatical or phonological development. McTear (1990) points out that as well as autistic and language impaired groups, there is another group of children who present only with a pragmatic/conversational disability. These children are typically diagnosed as having a semantic-pragmatic disorder, following Rapin and Allen's (1983) classification system which describes sub-groups of children exhibiting developmental language and communication disorders. In practice, it is often very difficult to differentiate between those children with autistic spectrum disorders, those with developmental language disorders and those with a purely pragmatic disorder. Of course the nature of the difficulty has significant implications for prognosis and for the way in which the child might respond to intervention.

The problem of differential diagnosis is further compounded because there are few standard assessments which enable the therapist to pinpoint areas of weakness and to establish a baseline level of functioning. Children with pragmatic/conversational difficulties generally score well on the linguistic assessments routinely used in the speech and language therapy clinic. Furthermore, in a quiet clinic with a sympathetic adult who will structure the conversation for him/her, the child may appear much more capable as a communicator than he/she really is. The real conversational abilities of these children are more likely to be revealed in natural communication settings. It makes sense therefore that this is where they should be assessed. It is important that the assessment takes account of the different circumstances in which the child has to converse. For example, the conversation will change according to the child's conversational partner, and the data gathered while the child is conversing with an adult who might use a variety of different strategies to compensate for the child's difficulties, may be quite different from that gathered when the child is trying to interact with his/her peers. In some practised and familiar situations, the child will know what is expected of him/her in the conversation, and the interaction may be much more effective and successful than in those situations where the child cannot predict how he/she is suppsed to respond. Some topics will be easier for the child to discuss than others, probably depending on their familiarity. All of these factors need to be taken into account.

If the child is to be assessed in more natural communicative contexts, thus allowing for the variables of partner, situation and topic, then the therapist needs some knowledge of the rules which govern normal conversation. When working with children with grammatical or phonological impairments, therapists apply their knowledge of the grammatical and phonological rules of the language to work out where there is a mismatch between those rules and what the child is doing. They also take account of normal developmental patterns to decide whether a feature is delayed or disordered. It would make sense to assess the conversational skills of those children with a pragmatic/concersational disability in the same way, and the framework of conversational analysis enables the therapist to do this. The therapist can scan data collected in natural communication settings for specific conversational skills and strategies in order to identify clinically significant features. The profile which emerges can be compared with what is already known about conversational develoment in children with normal language and children with autistic spectrum or with language disorders. It is also an approach which allows the selection of intervention goals based on linguistic analysis.

There has been little work done on the remediation of pragmatic difficulties. Some authors (Conti-Ramsden and Gunn 1986; Jones, Smedley and Jennings 1986; Hyde-Wright and Cray 1990) outline their approaches to the treatment of semantic pragmatic disorder, but the efficacy of therapy has not been demonstrated. The programmes of intervention described are not based on detailed linguistic analysis, and there is no description of baseline functioning or empirical evidence of measurable improvement.

In this paper, the principles of conversational analysis will be used to describe the communication of a child who was described as having a semantic-pragmatic disorder. It will be demonstrated that this method of assessment provided a profile of the child's conversational strategies based on detailed observation and linguistic analysis. Once a baseline profile was obtained, it was possible to select target areas for intervention, and then to re-assess the child to demonstrate qualitative and quantitative improvements in his conversation.

2.   The subject

N was the third child of two teachers. The family lived in the North of England, and was English speaking. N was four years younger than his twin brother and sister. He was born two weeks premature, following a difficult pregnancy during which his mother was hospitalised twice because of her high blood pressure. N's mother reported that his developmental milestones occurred later than his siblings', particularly in the area of speech and language. His hearing and vision were normal. At eighteen months, N was referred for a speech and language therapy assessment, as he was not using language to communicate and he exhibited some atypical behaviours, such as hand flapping and running around in circles. N attended a mainstream nursery from chronological age 3;4 to 4;8, and then he spent a year in a school for autistic children. He was transferred to a language unit at 5;8.

When he arrived at the language unit, N scored at an average or just below average level in formal assessments of his receptive language (Test for the Reception of Grammar, Bishop 1982; Reynell Developmental Language Scales, Reynell 1977). He was using the appropriate grammatical structures to command, question and comment. Nevertheless he found it very difficult to converse with others. His responses often did not relate to the preceding utterance, and he found it difficult to maintain a topic over a number of turns.

3.   Profile of Conversational Behaviours

Because N's difficulties with language did not show up in formal assessment tasks, a procedure was designed to analyse his conversational behaviours in a range of different situations (Willcox and Mogford-Bevan 1995a). Paper and pencil observations were made in different situations in the school (in the language unit classroom, in the mainstream class where N was integrated for part of the week, in the dining hall and in the playground). These observations detailed N's conversational partner, the topic of their conversation, the forms used in the interaction, and the linguistic and extra-linguistic context. N was also video-recorded at play with three different conversational partners (a familiar adult, a familiar peer and an unfamiliar peer). The recorded interactions were scanned for clinically significant conversational behaviours. Clear patterns of atypical conversational behaviours emerged in the following areas:

3.1 Attention Getting Devices

Attention getting devices or pre-sequences (Lesser and Milroy 1993) are used by the speakers to secure the attention of the listener. They usually occur as a three part sequence, which Lesser and Milroy describe as a summons-response-reason for summons sequence. The participants in conversation are oriented towards the third part of the sequence, and it is expected that the first speaker will fill that slot. Attention getting devices are realised as vocatives (e.g. "Mummy", "Mrs.

Smith", as notice verbs (e.g. "look", "watch") or in the form of non-lexical items (e.g. "hey", "oy"). They may also take the form of pre-announcements (e.g. "Do you know what..", "Do you remember..").

N did not appear to appreciate the significance of the three part sequence. Frequently, he did not use any attention getting device at all to alert the listener to attend to his subsequent utterance. Consequently potential addressees were not aware that they were being addressed, and did not respond to his initiations. On other occasions, N used an attention getting device, often another child's name, without following up the summons implication. Typically he would repeat the child's name several times, but did not fulfil his conversational obligation to provide the third part of the sequence i.e. the reason for the summons. N was also observed to use gaze to attract attention and was often noted to stare intently at a potential addressee before speaking to them.

3.2 *Initiations*

These are defined as utterances which start afresh and which set up the expectation of a response (Coulthard 1985).

As discussed above, N's initiations were not always preceded by an attention getting device, and consequently did not receive a reply, because N had not indicated who he was addressing.

Alternatively N often tried to start up a conversation using a form that did not demand a response from the addressee. N tended to use declarative forms to initiate, and there was therefore no obligation for his conversational partner to reply. N usually commented on what he was doing, or on what was happening around him rather than trying to engage the other person in a topic that might have been mutually interesting. The responsibility therefore of maintaining the interaction fell to N's conversational partner, who had to take up N's choice of topic. Adults were typically very good at identifying when N was trying to start up a conversation, but other children frequently failed to respond to N's declarative initiations.

N also used interrogatives to initiate. These forms did demand a response from the addressee, but N's questions were often difficult to answer. Sometimes it was clear that he already knew the answers to the questions himself. On other occasions, N's questions sounded unusual in the circumstances in which they were asked, and the addressee, although obliged to respond by the question form, found it difficult to do so.

3.3 *Directives*

The ability to manipulate the actions of others to achieve one's own ends is described by Halliday (1975) as being one of the first linguistic functions to evolve in very young children. However many of N's attempts to direct the actions of others were unsuccessful, because N used unusual grammatical forms to make a request. Typically N used a declarative when he wanted something. For example, when he wanted the teacher to mark his work, N said:

(1)   N: I done good work.

On Armistice Day, N made it clear from his actions (i.e. struggling to put a poppy in his jumper and looking pleadingly at an adult) that he wanted the adult to help him put the poppy in his jumper, but he said:

(2)   N: I got a poppy.

The use of a declarative is not in itself that unusual as a request — indeed many young children use declaratives to indicate what they want. N however seemed to be unaware that he could change the form of his request in order to make his intentions more explicit to the addressee. He lacked the flexibility to do this. It was interesting that adults generally responded to N's implicit requests, but other children did not.

N also rarely used the word "please" which might have helped to make his requests more explicit, as well as making them appear more polite.

3.4 *Responses*

Coulthard (1985) defines a response as an utterance which is predicted by the preceding utterance. A response does not necessarily itself set up expectations for further utterances. N characteristically presented with difficulties in fulfilling his conversational obligation to fill the response slots set up for him by his conversational partners.

N often appeared to be unaware of the utterances of his conversational partner, and he failed to respond at all. It was evident that his conversational partners were expecting a reply, because they repeated or rephrased their utterances in order to elicit one. For example here James (J) tried to find out what N watched on television:

(3)   J: _ _ _ _ do you watch Blue Peter?
              _ _ do you?
        N: no

Sometimes N recognised the repeated attempt by his conversational partner to get him to reply, and he filled the response slot. However there were occasions where his conversational partners had to repeatedly call him by name, or even touch him, before N was aware that he was being addressed, and that he was expected to reply. N also failed to respond to non-verbal initiations. For example, he rarely smiled back when another person smiled at him, but generally maintained a blank facial expression.

N frequently failed to demonstrate an appreciation of the organisation of discourse, and the tendency for conversation to be organised in closely related paired turns. Schegloff and Sacks (1973) describe these as adjacency pairs, where the first part of the pair sets up expectations about the second part of the pair. N frequently failed to meet the expectations of his conversational partner by contributing an utterance (the second part of the pair) that did not correspond with his partner's utterance (the first part of the pair).

3.5 *Cohesion*

N's difficulties with responding on topic had implications for his ability to take responsibility for maintaining the continuity of the conversation. However he did demonstrate some strategies for linking his utterances with those of his conversational partner.

He often repeated all or part of his conversational partner's utterance, as a means of agreeing with his partner, or of affirming what his partner had just said. Often an ellipted response or "yes" or "no" response would have been more usual. For example an adult was asking N here if a play person was too big to go in the front seat of the camper van. N used a full sentence to reply:

(4)   A: _ _ is he too big?
        N: he's too big.

N also used sentence connectives in a way which did not correspond with adult usage. He used sophisticated discourse connectives like "well", "actually" and "certainly" in a way which suggested that he did not fully understand their usage.

3.6 *Repair*

This term is used to describe the strategies that participants in conversation use in order to deal with mishearings and misunderstandings. N had difficulties dealing with breakdowns in communication, and he was apparently unaware of the mechanisms that are commonly used to sort out trouble spots in conversation.

Generally N relied on repetition to resolve conversational difficulties. For example, there were examples where N's conversational partner did not respond to N's initiations. In this kind of situation, repair is usually effected by the speaker making an attempt to get the attention of the addressee (e.g. by using an attention getting device) or by the speaker making syntactic alterations to the initiation in order to increase the obligations on the addressee to respond. N would simply repeat his utterance, without changing it, until he received a reply. Again this is not that unusual a strategy. What was unusual was that N continued to repeat himself, even if the first repetition failed to get a response. He seemed unaware of other strategies he could use to get the other person to reply. N also used repetition when other people requested clarification. Typically he would simply repeat his utterance in exactly the same form. Often this was sufficient to sort out the misunderstanding, but on other occasions N's conversational partner was still unable to establish what N was talking about.

4.   Intervention

The intervention procedures designed to improve N's communication are described in detail by Willcox and Mogford-Bevan (1995b). In this paper, only the changes which occurred in N's ability to respond to the initiations of others will be discussed, as this was an important factor contributing to N's isolation from his peers. There was an interesting contrast in the way in which N responded to adults and to other children. For example the percentage number of nil responses to the initiations of others was calculated (i.e. occasions where N did not respond at all to a comment, question or command explicitly directed to him by another speaker). N generally responded to adult initiations — in the observation assessment, he failed to respond to only 11% of adult initiations and in the video assessment, he failed to respond to 41% of the familiar adult's initiations. He was much less likely to respond to other children however. In the observation assessment, he ignored 50% of other children's attempts to initiate interaction. The percentage was even higher in the video assessment, where N failed to respond 61% of the familiar child's initiations, and 70% of the unfamiliar child's initiations. The percentages from the video assessments are particularly striking because N was alone with each of his conversational partners, and their initiations could not have been addressed to anyone else but him. Moreover the other children often worked very hard to elicit a reply from N, changing the grammatical structure of their initiations, and calling him by name to signal that he was being addressed. Qualitative analysis however suggested that the familiar adult was better able to compensate for N's unresponsiveness, and she designed her conversation to take account of N's difficulties. She accepted and responded to his utterances even when they only weakly demanded a response, and she followed up N's topic more readily rather than introducing topics of her own. She persisted in repeating and rephrasing questions until N responded to her satisfaction. She helped N to reply in question-answer sequences by giving him forced alternative and phonemic cues. The other children did not do this.

As part of a research project to demonstrate the efficacy of therapy, N was exposed to two different intervention programmes. The first addressed his use of directives, and was designed to encourage N to use a polar interrogative rather than a declarative when making a request. N was encouraged to use the word "please" and to use an attention getting device (the name of the addressee) as part of his request. A behavioural approach was adopted where N had to imitate a target structure, then was prompted to use it, and then was required to use it spontaneously before getting a reward. The second intervention programme was specifically designed to address N's failure to respond to the intiations of others. A meta-linguistic approach was adopted, and N worked with a group of other children and discussed and practised good conversation strategies. In this group, N learned to respond to greetings and partings and to smiles. He was made aware of the non-verbal and verbal methods of demonstrating that he was listening, and was encouraged to respond on topic.

In subsequent re-assessment, there was a dramatic change in the percentage of nil responses with different conversational partners. N was re-assessed using exactly the same procedure of observation and video recording, and the data was scanned in the same way for significant conversational features. In the observation re-assessment, the percentage of nil responses to adult initiations remained relatively constant at 10%. The percentage of nil responses to the advances of other children however was significantly reduced to 14%. This change was mirrored in the video data, where again there was a slight improvement in the adult interaction (from 41% to 31%), but a big improvement in the peer interaction. N failed to respond to only 14% of the familiar child's initiations, and 16% of the unfamiliar child's initiations.

Obviously the quantitative results reveal nothing about the quality of N's interactions. However a qualitative examination of the data reinforced the numerical findings. In the first assessment, N often rejected or ignored the communicative overtures of other children. When he did respond to them, his replies often bore little relation to what the other child had just said. In re-assessment, it was clear that N was much more interested in what other children were saying or doing, and used conversation as a means of expressing that interest. He started to share in play activities, and to respond to and maintain conversation about them.

The other interesting feature was that there was a marked increase in the number of occasions where other children approached N. In the observation assessment, the total numer of other child initiations almost doubled in re-assessment. There are two possible explanations for this. During assessment and intervention, there had been much adult time and energy spent with N, and there is a body of research that suggests that if high prestige members of a community (i.e. the adults in a school environment) favour an individual, then that individual will also be favoured by other members of the community. Alternatively, the increase could be explained by the change in N's communicative behaviour. N actively started to join in with games and conversations initiated by other children, and began to converse and play in a more reciprocal way. Conversations had become more co-operative, and were as intrinsically reinforcing for N's peers as they were for N. It appeared that following intervention, N was caught in a positive cycle where his conversational behaviour was constantly being reinforced by his peers.

5. Discussion

As an assessment tool, the framework provided by conversational analysis proved very effective indeed. The case study of N indicates that using a conversational analysis approach allows the therapist to look at the child in a range of contexts and with a range of partners. It became very clear how important it was to do this. For example, N's communication was indeed enhanced, as predicted, when he was interacting with adults, who normalised and accepted his contributions in a way that his peers did not. Likewise his attempts to interact were noted to be much better in familiar settings (e.g. the language unit classroom) than in less familiar and therefore safer environments (e.g. the mainstream classroom and the playground). To consider N in all these environments, was clearly vital.

The process of conversational analysis also focused the therapist on the rules governing conversation. It was possible to identify which rules N regularly failed to appreciate, and to describe his own idiosyncratic rules. It was then possible to target specific behaviours and to teach N more normal strategies. The framework of conversational analysis implies that conversational behaviours are independent of one another and can be assessed and treated as such. In fact, the study demonstrated how closely the conversational behaviours were interrelated, and that intervention focusing on one behaviour was found to have effects on other behaviours. For example, the therapy focusing on N's requesting behaviour was found to have had an effect on his ability to respond in conversation, in that, following the initial intervention programme, the number of nil or inappropriate responses decreased. It could be argued that in learning to use an interrogative to request, N learned something of the obligations of conversation. An interrogative signals to the listener that he/she needs to reply. Learning to use interrogatives to make a request, and learning to expect a response, N also may have begun to realise that he was required to respond himself in conversation. This area was then selected as the next target in therapy, to see whether further improvements could be effected, as indeed they were.

Many of the conversational behaviours exhibited by N also have been observed in much younger children who are developing language normally. N used declaratives to initiate interaction, and to make requests. Craig and Gallagher (1979) found that 71% of the dialogue utterances of 2–3 year olds were declarative in form, and Ervin-Tripp (1977) reports that "need statements" or declaratives are the first form of directive used by young children. N's failure to respond or to respond on topic is noted by Piaget (1926) as a feature of egocentric speech, where the child's contributions to the conversation relate only to his/her previous utterance. Keenan and Schieffelin (1976) note that very young children are often so absorbed in their own activities that they fail to respond to their conversational partner's utterances. N frequently repeated all or part of his conversational partner's utterances as a means of acknowledging what his partner had said, and also in response to clarification requests. Repetition is often used in early mother-child and child-child interactions as a device to maintain topic (Keenan 1974, Ochs-Keenan 1977), as a means of renegotiating a failed initiation (Keenan and Schieffelin 1976, Atkinson 1979) and as a response to clarification requests (Gallagher 1977, Brinton, Fujiki, Frome-Loeb and Winkler 1986). It could be argued that N presented with a severe delay rather than a disorder in his conversational development. The combination of immature conversational behaviours, combined with mature grammatical and phonological forms, accounts for N's impaired communication. This is similar to other areas of language impairment, where children with grammatical and phonological disabilities often demonstrate the grammatical and phonological characteristics of much younger children. It would be theoretically elegant to suggest that the same is true for children with conversational/pragmatic difficulties. There is a need for more research to establish whether other children with conversational/pragmatic disabilities exhibit similar conversational behaviours to N, and thus whether this hypothesis is correct.

Further research would also be necessary to establish whether the profile provided by conversational analysis could be used as a tool in differential diagnosis. That there are several groups of children who present with conversational/pragmatic disabilities has already been discussed. N's response to therapy, and his subsequent improvement suggests that he had a conversational/pragmatic disability in the absence of a grammatical or an autistic disorder. More research needs to be done to see whether children with grammatical difficulties exhibit different conversational behaviours and strategies to N. It would also be interesting to see whether children with autistic spectrum disorders exhibit different behaviours from these other groups, or indeed if children with autism behave differently from children with Asperger's syndrome when they are engaged in conversation.

6.   Conclusion

The process of conversational analysis provided the therapist with a framework within which it was possible to identify specific and recurring problems in N's interaction in a range of communicative contexts. It was possible to describe why N found it difficult to sustain meaningful conversation with others, and to describe what was atypical about his conversational behaviour. It was also possible to target specific behaviours, and to teach N more normal strategies. In addition, the approach enabled the therapist to demonstrate both qualitative and quantitative improvements in N's interaction. These are powerful arguments for the adoption of this approach in the routine assessment of children with pragmatic/conversational difficulties.

Acknowledgements

The authors would like to thank N's family, and the staff at his school. The authors are also grateful to North Durham Community Health Care Trust for facilitating this research. Some of the material discussed here has already appeared in Willcox and Mogford-Bevan (1995b).

References

Atkinson, M. 1979. "Pre-requisites for reference". In *Developmental Pragmatics*, E. Ochs and B. Schieffelin (eds). New York: Academic Press.

Bishop, D. V. M. 1982. *Test for the Reception of Grammar*. Medical Research Council.

Brinton, B. and Fujiki, M. 1982. "A comparison of request-response sequences in the discourse of normal and language impaired children". *Journal of Speech and Hearing Research* 47: 57–62.

Brinton, B., Fujiki, M., Frome-Loeb, D. and Winkler, E. 1986. "Development of conversational repair strategies in response to requests for clarification". *Journal of Speech and Hearing Research* 29 (1): 75–81.

Conti-Ramsden, G. and Friel-Patti, S. 1983. "Mothers' discourse adjustments to language impaired and non-language impaired children". *Journal of Speech and Hearing Disorders* 48: 360–367.

Conti-Ramsden, G. and Gunn, M. 1986. "The development of conversational disability: a case study". *British Journal of Disorders of Communication* 21: 339–351.

Coulthard, R. M. 1985. *An Introduction to Discourse Analysis*. London: Longman.

Craig, H. K. and Evans, T. M. 1989. "Turn exchange characteristics of SLI children's simultaneous and nonsimultaneous speech". *Journal of Speech and Hearing Disorders* 54: 334–47.

Craig, H. and Gallagher, T. M. 1979. "The structural characteristics of monologues in the speech of normal children: syntactic non-conversational aspects". *Journal of Speech and Hearing Research* 22: 46–62.

Donahue, M., Pearl, R. and Bryan, T. 1980. "Learning disabled children's conversational competence: responses to adequate messages". *Applied Psycholinguistics* 1: 387–403.

Ervin-Tripp, S. 1977. "Wait for me, roller skate". In *Child Discourse*, S. Ervin-Tripp and C. Mitchell-Kernan (eds). New York: Academic Press.

Fey, M. E. and Leonard, L. B. 1983. "Pragmatic skills of children with specific language impairment". In *Pragmatic Assessment and Intervention Issues in Language*, T. M. Gallagher and C. A. Prutting (eds). San Diego: College Hill Press.

Gallagher, T. M. 1977. "Revision behaviors in the speech of normal children developing language". *Journal of Speech and Hearing Research* 20: 303–18.

Gallagher, T. M. and Darnton, B. A. 1978. "Conversational aspects of the speech of language impaired children: revision behaviors". *Journal of Speech and Hearing Research* 21: 118–135.

Halliday, M. A. K. 1975. *Learning How to Mean: Explorations in the Development of Language*. London: Edward Arnold.

Hyde-Wright, S. and Cray, B. 1990. "A teacher's and a speech therapist's approach to management". In *Child Language Disability Vol II: Semantic and Pragmatic Difficulties*, K. Mogford-Bevan and J. Saddler (eds). Clevedon: Multilingual Matters.

Jones, S., Smedley, M. and Jennings, M. 1986. "Case study: a child with high level language disorder characterised by syntactic, semantic and pragmatic difficulties". In *Advances in Working with Language Disordered Children*, Invalid Children's Aid Nationwide (eds). London: ICAN.

Keenan, E. 1974. "Conversational competence in children". *Journal of Child Language* 1: 163–183.

Keenan, E. and Schieffelin, B. 1976. "Topic as a discourse notion: a study of topic in the conversation of children and adults". In *Subject and Topic*, C. Li (ed.). New York: Academic Press.

Lesser, R. and Milroy, L. 1993. *Linguistics and Aphasia: Psycholinguistic and Pragmatic Aspects of Intervention.* London: Longman.

McTear, M. F. 1990. "Is there such a thing as conversational disability". In *Child Language Disability Vol II: Semantic and Pragmatic Difficulties*, K. Mogford-Bevan and J. Saddler (eds). Clevedon: Multilingual Matters.

Ochs-Keenan, E. 1977. "Making it last: repetition in children's discourse". In *Child Discourse*, S. Ervin-Tripp and C. Mitchell-Kernan (eds). New York: Academic Press.

Piaget, J. 1926. *The Language and Thought of the Child.* London: Routledge and Kegan-Paul.

Rapin, A. and Allen, D. 1983. "Developmental language disorders: nosologic considerations". In *Neuropsychology of Language, Reading and Spelling*, U. Kirk (ed). New York: Academic Press.

Reynell, J. K. 1977. *Reynell Developmental Language Scales.* Windsor: NFER-Nelson.

Rutter, M. 1978. "Diagnosis and definition in childhood autism". *Journal of Autism and Developmental Disorders* 8: 139–161.

Schegloff, E. A. and Sacks, H. 1973. "Openings and closings". *Semiotica* 7: 289–327.

Willcox, A. H. E. and Mogford-Bevan, K. 1995a. "Assessing conversational disability." *Clinical Linguistics and Phonetics* 9 (3): 235–254.

Willcox, A. H. E. and Mogford-Bevan, K. 1995b. "Conversational disability: assessment and remediation". In *Case Studies in Clinical Linguistics*, M. Perkins and S. Howard (eds). London: Whurr.

Wing, L. 1981. "Asperger's syndrome: a clinical account". *Psychological Medicine* 11: 115–130.

Wing, L. 1988. "The continuum of autistic characteristics". In *Diagnosis and Assessment in Autism*, E. Schopler and G. B. Mesibov (eds). New York: Plenum.

The Pragmatics of Paediatric Language Intervention

Issues and Analysis

Stephen M. Camarata
Vanderbilt University Medical Centre

1. Introduction and Background

The purpose of this chapter is to examine the pragmatic aspects of a number of widely used paediatric language intervention programs. Although the focus of intervention is often on the structural aspects of language (Camarata, Nelson, and Camarata 1994; Fey 1986; Fey, Windsor and Warren 1995; Lahey 1988), the actual intervention is completed within a social context with its own set of pragmatic parameters. These parameters vary considerably across treatment types and may also diverge substantially from the contexts associated with natural language learning (Moerk 1992) or with other learning contexts (e.g. preschool). The pragmatic characteristics of six intervention procedures used commonly and drawn from a diverse range of theoretical orientations will be reviewed below.

In addition, the treatments reviewed above do not include direct teaching of metalinguistic or metapragmatic skills. In young children, through early school age (i.e., into first or second grade; approximately 8;0), the focus of intervention is often on establishing use of linguistic structures. After the child enters school, the focus of intervention often shifts to metalinguistic, and for those children with pragmatic disabilities, to metapragmatic teaching approaches (Lahey 1988). The review of procedures in this chapter will be limited to procedures focusing on the preschool to early school age populations (and thus exclude metalinguistic/metapragmatic protocols).

In order to complete this review, one must first adopt a framework for examining the pragmatic characteristics of an intervention. Given the variability in pragmatic analysis schemes available currently (Ball, this volume; Conti-

Ramsden 1990; Prutting and Kirchner 1987), and the fundamentally different assumptions surrounding the role of pragmatics in language acquisition (e.g. Bates 1976), the framework selected for this chapter will be described in this section. At issue is the selection of the best means for characterizing the social context associated with the clinical procedures under study. Webster's Third International Dictionary (1969) includes the following definition of pragmatics: "a branch of semiotics that deals with the relation between signs or linguistic expressions and their users." Although this definition captures the essence of pragmatics, it is insufficient to generate a concise set of analyses to evaluate the social use of language in the clinical contexts (as can be seen in Ball, this volume). Indeed, it could be argued that the parameters measured in experimental contexts may not capture key aspects of the social behaviors observed clinically (see Prutting and Kirchner 1987). This may be due in part to the divergent goals of research and clinical practice: the former is often concerned with detailed descriptions of relatively narrowly defined parameters, whereas the latter is often concerned with more global judgements of adequacy in everyday communicative environments.

Thus, from a broad perspective, one must first decide to adopt an integrated, formalist or functionalist, figure-ground position on pragmatics (Owens 1991; Prutting 1979). The formalist, integrated perspective places the pragmatic domain as one of the integrated parts of language. For example, Camarata (1991) describes language as a interaction among phonologic, semantic, syntactic, morphologic, and pragmatic domains. Crystal (1987) proposes several 'levels' of language domains that include those described in Camarata, but with additional components such as phonemic and phonetic levels in addition to a prosodic component (which are subsumed under phonology). Similarly, Bloom and Lahey (1978) present an integrated coordination of content, form, and use (use in this case relates to the pragmatic domain) as the basis for language. In short, the formalist perspective focuses on the social use of language as window into the child's acquisition (and competence) of language structure.

In contrast, the functionalist perspective places social interaction (and pragmatic context) at the root of language, as the basis for communication (Bates and McWhinney 1989, also chapters, this volume). These assumptions of course have direct implications on how pragmatic analysis is conducted. The formalist approaches result in lists of communicative behavior observed during conversation (Dore 1974; Miller 1981; Prutting and Kirchner 1987, Prutting 1979; Leonard, Camarata, Schwartz, Rowan and Chapman 1982) whereas functionalist approaches result in detailed descriptions of the context surrounding and supporting communication (Bloom 1993; Prutting 1979). Thus, to complete a pragmatic analysis of the treatment context, one could classify the ways that children and clinicians use the various pragmatic structures reported in the literature (e.g. the Pragmatic Protocol, Prutting and Kirchner 1987) and/or one could examine the social contexts that serve as the backdrop for intervention.

Given my previous adoption of a formalist perspective in modeling language (Camarata 1991) and in intervention studies (Camarata 1993; Camarata and Nelson 1992; Camarata et al. 1994), it is ironic that the pragmatic review in this chapter will, although it will include formal elements, be completed primarily from a functionalist perspective. This choice is predicated upon the basic characteristics of intervention activities which, even in the most 'naturalistic' types, arise from the social context of delivering clinical services to the child. In a sense, the clinical motivation serves as the background for clinical activities, in much the same manner as functionalists argue that communication arises from the social context (Searle 1969). Thus, the pragmatics of language interventions can perhaps be best viewed as arising from a set of principles underlying the basic assumptions of the intervention. In this sense, the pragmatic context is, unlike many conversational contexts, under the direct or indirect control of the clinician. Stated simply, the social context of the intervention is the direct by-product of the type of intervention selected; a situation that is perhaps best examined within a functionalist perspective. Therefore, for the purposes of this chapter, pragmatics will be defined as the description of the social aspects of the language interaction between the clinician and the child during intervention activities. What follows is a commentary on the dynamics of this interaction and a comparison to the kinds of social interaction the child is likely to encounter in conversations outside of the clinic. As noted above, the evaluation of the individual treatments will be completed using a functionalist approach. This will thus involve a description of the treatment procedures and a detailed description and analysis of the social context for each treatment.

2. Treatment Orientations

There have been a rather large number of treatments for paediatric language disorders from an equally large number of theoretical orientations proposed in the past few decades (cf. Fey 1986). These range from unconscious conflicts within a Freudian perspective (Wyatt 1969); environmental deprivation (Curtiss 1977); faulty learning from a Skinnerian perspective (McReynolds 1987); defects in the child's information processing skills (Kirk and Kirk 1971) and/or neuro-logical system (Myklebust 1971; Benton 1964; Plante, Swisher, Vance and Rapcak 1991; Aram 1988); to genetic defects (Pinker 1995; Tomblin 1989). Not surprisingly, these different positions on causality often translate into strikingly different intervention procedures. For example, therapy completed using traditional operant learning procedures (Skinner 1957) bears little resemblance to treatment arising from more cognitivist perspectives (Muma 1978). However, despite these differences, it is possible to classify interventions into more general categories. For example, Fey (1986) used clinician oriented, child oriented, and hybrid designations. Camarata (1995; 1996), wishing to avoid operant and cognitivist classifications in his review of phonological treatments used a functional "analog/didactic" and "naturalistic" dichotomy.

Because the focus of this chapter is on the social context surrounding treatment, while examining a wide range of approaches, this dichotomy is expanded to include six representative interventions. These range from the most direct type of analog/didactic treatment founded upon traditional operant proce-dures to 'whole language' procedures which are the functional antithesis to analog procedures (Norris 1990; Norris and Hoffman 1993). Ordinal subdivision of these poles includes incidental teaching, milieu teaching, natural language paradigm, conversational recast procedures, and whole language. Each was selected to represent a shift from the high degree of clinician control associated with didactic methods towards the high levels of child control in whole language methods. It is important to note that this range is predicated upon characteristics of the treatments rather than adoption of a particular causal basis for the language disorder. It is clear that different assumptions about causality can result in similar treatment contexts. For example, the operant perspectives of McReynolds and the government-binding theories of Chomsky (1982) as implemented by Connell and Stone (1992), arise from very different theoretical frameworks, and include orthogonal perspectives on target selection, nonetheless are highly similar regarding the actual treatment context. Similarly, identical assumptions regarding causality can result in remarkably different treatment contexts. For example, Camarata et al. (1994), and Kirk and Kirk (1971) adopt an information processing perspective on language disorders, yet the former have adopted a conversation based intervention procedure whereas the latter include traditional didactic procedures. Thus, the procedures reviewed below are based upon the treatment context rather than on the position the authors have adopted regarding causality.

3. Analog/Didactic Imitation Based Intervention

3.1 *Description of the Intervention*

As noted above, analog/didactic treatment is rooted in traditional operant methodology (Skinner 1957). This has been a widely used procedure (Camarata *et al.* 1994; Fey 1986) and could be said to be the foundation for an entire class of intervention methods with operant underpinnings. Perhaps the most straightforward presentation of this procedure is the Monterey Language Program (Gray and Ryan 1973). The focus of analog treatment is the elicitation and reinforcement of targeted language structures. In order to do this, the clinician selects relevant goals (see Connell 1987 for a discussion of goal selection for this approach), and elicits production in a series of programmed steps designed to provide maximum saliency and behavioral support for initial production followed by a systematic fading of these supports and increasing delays and flexibility in reinforcement schedules (and reinforcers) as the child successfully produces the selected target(s). For example, assume the target is the auxiliary form "is" (e.g. "the boy is running"). In the analog/didactic approach, the clinician presents a picture representation of the target and a model "the boy is running" followed by a request for direct imitation "say the boy is running." If the child correctly imitates the model, verbal and/or tangible reinforcers are delivered. If the child's production is incorrect, feedback is provided in the form of verbal instructions and withholding the reward. When the child reaches a preset level of correct responses (of a percentage of overall attempts), the imitative prompt is faded. After the criteria for this level has been achieved, the model is also faded and so on until the child reaches generalized production that is minimally supported by clinician cues, prompts, and reinforcers. Although this paradigm was developed and adopted several decades ago, elements of this approach continue to be used widely in clinical settings with a variety of treatment targets (e.g., focused imitation was a part of the clinician training condition within Fey, Cleave and Long 1997, and imitation continues to be used extensively with phonological goals; see Camarata 1995, 1996). Note that this approach has been used widely with a wide variety of disability typologies, including specific language impairment, children with developmental delays, children with autism, and children with hearing impairments (see the review in Fey 1986).

3.2 *Example of Clinical Interaction*

This approach is often completed while the child and the clinician are seated at a table. Materials typically include photos depicting target sentences. Real objects (e.g., toys) are also included if appropriate. To initiate a teaching episode, the clinician shows the child a picture or object. In this example, assume the target is the auxiliary form of "be".

(1)   Clinician Look, the boy is running. Say: The boy is running.
       Child   (incorrect response) boy running
       Clinician (no reinforcer is delivered) No, say: The boy IS running.
                (with added emphasis on the target.)
       Child   (correct response) The boy is running.
       Clinician (delivers token reinforcement) Yes, good!

In subsequent sessions, the clinician model and prompt are faded.

(2)   Clinician (shows picture) Look at this!
       Child   The boy is running.
       Clinician (delivers token) Yes, good!

Then, the clinician fades the reinforcers so that the child says the target form in response to being shown the picture (or object). Token reinforcers include coins, plastic chips, or markers that can be exchanged for small toys or stickers at the end of the treatment session.

3.3 Pragmatic Aspects of the Intervention

Consider the child-clinician interaction from a functionalist pragmatic perspective: the context for the interaction often includes a small room in a clinic. The clinician exercises relatively tight control over stimuli in order to provide maximum salience and support for elicited production of the targets. In addition, materials are selected and presented by the clinician. From a conversational perspective, the goal of the interaction is direct imitation of the clinician model and few features of typical conversations are present in the clinician-child interaction. Thus, the pragmatic aspects of didactic/analog intervention include almost exclusively directives from the clinician and responses from the child, particularly during the initial phases of intervention.

As the child progresses through treatment, the clinician directives shift from verbal to nonverbal, but the primary context and conversational expectations remain; the child is expected to produce targets in response to clinician provided cues. Another pragmatic aspect of analog/didactic intervention relates to the delivery of verbal reinforcers. The pragmatic character of these shifts the context, from responding to directives to a metalinguistic focus on the accuracy of the child's imitated response. To summarize, the analog/didactic intervention includes few conversational elements and the purpose of the interaction is to elicit imitated production from the child.

In our own clinic, the analog/didactic approach has sometimes been associated with interesting errors in the child's production during spontaneous attempts. That is, the focus on production of forms in the context of clinician directives exclusively may result in attention to the targeted structures without knowledge of function. The exchanges below, observed in our clinic, illustrate this result. In the following sequence, the language target was full propositional complement (e.g., I know who lives in that house). In this game, the clinician models the target and the child provides an answer. Then the child is required to produce the target with new words (this is a generalization phase).

(3)   Clinician I know what lives in the tree.
       Child   Monkeys!
       Child   I know who lives in the cat.
       Clinician What?
       Child   No, I know who lives in the police woman.
       Clinician What?
       Child   I said that word!

This example suggests that the child was attending to the form without regard to the meaning of the target phrase. At this point in acquisition, the child is producing the target correctly from a grammatical standpoint while making mistakes in meaning. We have observed this type of error only within analog/didactic treatments.

3.4 Relationship to Pragmatics of Generalization

This section is devoted to the comparison of the pragmatic aspects of the intervention to a more generalized context; spontaneous language in a variety of natural (versus clinical) contexts. Indeed, perhaps the strongest test of the effectiveness of the intervention is whether the targets are used in spontaneous language samples in generalization settings such as the home and/or school while talking to peers, siblings, and parents and other adult relatives. A further test of generalization is whether the child uses the targets in a variety of pragmatic roles; across settings, across conversation partners, and appropriately across formal pragmatic categories (e.g. in topics, responses, answers, requests, etc.).

From this perspective, there appears to be little overlap between the training context and the generalization context. Brown and Hanlon (1970) observed few overt, didactic/analog teaching episodes in a review of mother–child samples. Indeed, the relative infrequency of such episodes in normal language acquisition has prompted a shift in the operant accounts of language acquisition (see Bohannon and Warren-Leubecker 1989; Moerk 1992). However, it should be noted that the focus of didactic/analog intervention is squarely on elicited production because of the belief that the child will generalize to the ambient context if a target is added to the production repertoire. Before this assumption is dismissed (and this entire section is simply viewed as a "straw man"), it is important to note that although there have been numerous reports of difficulty in achieving generalized use of targets learned under didactic/analog approaches (see Fey 1986; Koegel, O'Dell, and Koegel 1987); several reports (including our own work: Camarata *et al.* 1994; Nelson, Camarata, Welsh, Butkowski, and Camarata 1996) have revealed that children with specific language impairments sometimes learn and use targets in spontaneous language samples under didactic/analog training conditions. Indeed, Connell and Stone (1992) argue that direct imitation is the most efficient procedure for treating children with specific language impairment. Thus, in some cases, it appears that establishing productivity via imitation is sufficient for generalization to occur despite the pragmatic mismatch between the learning conditions and the generalization contexts. However, regardless of one's theoretical orientation, all agree it is clear that didactic/analog approaches intersect the generalized conversation context at very few points. The entire treatment context is designed to be dissimilar in order to highlight targets that the child is having difficulty learning in home and school contexts.

4. Incidental Teaching

4.1 *Description of the Intervention*

This approach was developed in order to teach language skills in contexts that more closely parallel the child's typical language use setting. First developed by Hart and Risley (1968), it has been recently updated and continues to be used in the United States, particularly in Special Education (Hart and Risley 1995). Because the program has been evolving over the past 30 years, it is difficult to incorporate all elements in a summary description of this type. However, it is perhaps reasonable to describe the approach as including the embedding of prompts, cues, and reinforcers into contexts wherein toys and other desired objects are controlled by the clinician in order to promote language production in the child. In the early versions of incidental teaching, the toys were placed outside the child's reach and were delivered only if the child imitated the targeted language form correctly (Hart, Reynolds, Baer, Brawley and Harris 1968; Hart and Risley 1968). It is also important to note that two of the approaches described below, milieu teaching and natural language paradigm are related to this approach and, in the case of milieu teaching, arose directly from the incidental teaching paradigm (Warren and Kaiser 1986; Warren, McQuarters and Rogers-Warren 1984). For the purposes of this discussion, the key elements of this approach include clinician prompting, requests for imitation and the delivery of social and, in some versions, tangible reinforcers within a context that includes toys and, in some versions, play activities. This approach, and milieu teaching, have been completed primarily with children with developmental disabilities (see Kaiser 1993).

4.2 *Example of Clinical Interaction*

In this intervention, desired objects are arranged so that the child cannot reach them. For example (adapted from Hart and Risley 1968; Hart and Rogers-Warren 1978), assume the targets for the following example include color names and requests. The clinician provides paint brushes and paper on the table in front of the child, but ensures that the paints are out of reach on a shelf above the table (but in view of the child).

(4)   Clinician Let's paint a picture.
        Child   (gestures to paints)
        Clinician What do you want? Say: I want the blue paint.
        Child   Paint, want paint.
        Clinician Say: I want the blue paint.

If the child says the full target, or an appropriate approximation ("I want the blue paint," or "blue paint"), the clinician delivers the requested object (in this case a can of blue paint) and may also include a social reinforcer ("good talking"). If the child does not respond correctly, the clinician may shorten the target phrase ("say: blue paint"), or direct the child's attention to another object. This sequence continues until the child is successful in producing the target or an acceptable approximation.

4.3 *Pragmatic Aspects of the Intervention*

Because the primary focus within incidental teaching remains on inducing production of key language targets, the social context in many ways closely parallels analog/didactic approaches. The clinician retains relatively exclusive control of the conversational dynamics: inducing the child to produce the language targets and delivering corrective feedback and/or reinforcers following child responses. As with the analog/didactic approach, the focus of the intervention is not on typical conversation, and interaction between the clinician and child is primarily model-direct request on the part of the clinician, followed by imitative response by the child and metalinguistic feedback by the clinician. However, unlike analog/didactic training, incidental teaching is conducted in play contexts, or minimally in contexts wherein toys and other play objects are included in training.

4.4   Relationship to Pragmatics of Generalization

The above analysis of incidental teaching suggests that it shares many of the pragmatic characteristics of analog/didactic treatment, including overt models and direct requests for imitation and overt social and/or tangible reinforcement. As noted above for analog/didactic training, relatively few of these types of episodes are present in the child's everyday language exchanges. However, unlike analog/didactic training, incidental teaching does include toys and play contexts and overlaps the pragmatic characteristics of the generalization setting in a number of ways, particularly in the request of objects. In analog/didactic approaches, object names are often trained as a learned response to picture and/or object stimuli presented to the child in terms of confrontation naming. For example, the clinician might show the child a picture of a ball or present a ball to the child and pair this with a model and a request for imitation: "Look, ball. Say: ball". In contrast, incidental teaching approaches often include placing the ball out of the child's reach and presenting the model and the request for imitation when the child shows interest in playing with the ball (cf. Hart and Risley 1968). The stated rationale for this includes increased motivation for production of the object name in a requesting social context (termed "mands" in the operant literature; Mowrer 1984).

Consider the functional pragmatics of this type of teaching episode: the child demonstrates, either verbally or nonverbally, that an out of reach object is desired, and the clinician provides a model and request for imitation in response to this request. This closely parallels important pragmatic aspects of the generalization context; mothers often respond to a child's request for an object with an object label (although a following request for imitation is less common, see Conti-Ramsden 1990; Moerk 1992). Perhaps not surprisingly, incidental teaching is very successful when attempting to train use of mands (Hart and Risley 1995). It should be noted that less overlap between incidental teaching and generalization contexts is evident in other pragmatic aspects. Interestingly, the incidental teaching approach has often been less successful when teaching language forms other than mands (see the review of incidental teaching in Fey 1986 and in Camarata, 1991).

5.   Milieu Teaching

5.1   *Description of the Intervention*

Milieu teaching was directly developed from incidental teaching, primarily by students of Hart and Risley (particularly Kaiser and Warren). This approach includes the basic elements of incidental teaching (i.e. models and requests for imitation), but also includes increased flexibility in modeling (and prompting imitation) of other types of child productions. Recent versions (Kaiser and Hester 1994) of milieu teaching include interacting with the child in play contexts while the clinician selects a set of developmentally appropriate language goals to model (and elicit) during play. In addition to the mand contexts used in incidental teaching (and described above), milieu teaching includes models and imitation requests that involve additions to a child's immediately preceding productions. That is, milieu teaching episodes include a broader range of activities and training contexts. Expansions, wherein the clinician follows the child's production with a model and a request for imitation as part of the training context are also used (e.g., if the child says "ball roll," a clinician could expand the utterance by adding grammatical morphemes such as progressive, auxiliary *be*, and definite article: "the ball is rolling"). Additional more 'naturalistic' (see Camarata 1996) elements are included as well.

For example, assume that a child's goal includes two word action-object semantic relations. The child and clinician are engaged in play activities that make use of toys that can be 'rolled' such as a ball, car, truck, train, toy tires, etc. In this approach the child would have some control of the toys and the clinician would model (and request for imitation) a number of different contingencies. The clinician could initiate the interaction by moving the car and prompting the child to produce "roll car." Alternatively, the child could initiate the action (by rolling the car) and the clinician model and prompt could follow the child's play engagement. Also, the model and prompt can be delivered following the child's verbal production of one or more elements in the target

structure (e.g. the child rolls a ball and says "roll," the clinician follows with
"roll ball; say: roll ball."). Thus, milieu teaching includes delivery of a model and
request for imitation as contingencies to a variety of child and clinician behaviors.

5.2 *Example of Clinical Interaction*

In this example, assume the setting and targets are similar to those described above
for the example for incidental teaching: Paint brushes and papers have been placed
in front of the child but the paints have been placed out of reach in plain sight.

> (5)   Clinician Let's paint a picture.
>   Child   (gestures to paints)
>   Clinician What?
>   Child   Paint.
>   Clinician Oh, you want the paint! Say, I want the blue paint.
>   Child   Paint, want paint
>   Clinician Yes, you want the paint. (gives paint to child) Here's the
>   blue paint; say: blue paint.

In this episode, the clinician reacts more directly to the child's production and
delivers the model as an expansion of the child's initial attempt. This flexibility
to respond to the child's attempt and deliver the model and imitative prompt is
viewed as an important modification of previous intervention procedures (Fey
1986; Kaiser 1993).

5.3 *Pragmatic Aspects of the Intervention*

Because the clinician is free to deliver models and requests for imitation in a
variety of contingent contexts, the pragmatic aspects of milieu teaching are much
more diverse than either analog/didactic or incidental teaching procedures. That
is, the clinician can be the initiator of the interaction (as in analog/didactic and
incidental teaching), or can respond to child requests and/or questions. This
flexibility allows for teaching episodes in divergent pragmatic contexts. Internal
analysis of the teaching episodes themselves indicates that the delivery of models
and requests for imitation are highly similar to the parameters described above
for incidental teaching: the clinician overtly directs the child's attention to the
target form and requests immediate imitation of the form. However, this internally
consistent form is delivered in play settings initiated by the clinician or the child.
Thus, the immediate pragmatic structure includes a model that is now more directly
linked to the play setting and a request for imitation that closely follows the model.

5.4   *Relationship to Pragmatics of Generalization*

As with the procedures reviewed above (analog/didactic and incidental teaching), milieu teaching includes direct instruction techniques that are not used widely in the generalization or naturalistic learning context. That is, because it is built upon similar model and prompt foundations, milieu teaching shares a number of functional pragmatic characteristics with these approaches. But milieu teaching provides these teaching episodes in contexts that occur naturally. The underlying theory is that embedding the teaching episodes into the play contexts will result in a closer association between the learned targets and the generalization settings, and allow the child to more easily make the transition to using the targets outside of the teaching episodes (Kaiser 1993). As Bambara and Warren (1993) observe, true generalization to spontaneous language is rarely measured directly and requires training that is flexible (and that parallels the generalization context). Milieu teaching is designed to be flexible and to promote more rapid generalization.

6.   Natural Language Paradigm

6.1   *Description of the Intervention*

Although the natural language paradigm (Koegel *et al.* 1987) shares many of the features and theoretical origins of milieu teaching, the approach warrants more detailed discussion because it directly focuses on motivating children with autism to communicate. That is, the procedure was developed specifically to improve the language skills of children with autism. This is of interest for a review of the pragmatic aspects of treatment because the motivation for communication is not addressed directly in most intervention approaches (see Camarata *et al.* 1994). Koegel *et al.* (1987) recognized that children with autism are not motivated to communicate (or engage in social interaction at all) and also applied functional analysis technology (Carr and Durand 1985) to determine which aspects of parent-child interactions would be communicative, and builds upon these interactions to expand the child's language. The first step in natural language paradigm is to determine whether the child uses any social interactions whatsoever. In most cases, even children that are almost totally antisocial will display some use of communicative behavior (although these behaviors may not be the usual forms of social interaction, as in the social use of echolalia; Prizant *et al.* 1993). After determining when the child is using social interaction and in which contexts these interactions occur (and what forms they take), a plan is developed to shape these productions into forms that are more useful and intelligible. The actual shaping includes the use of 'natural reinforcers' (that is desired objects in the play environment), and prompting.

This approach is distinct from analog/didactic, incidental teaching, and milieu teaching in a number of ways, but particularly regarding the nature of prompts: direct imitation is not used, rather the child is reinforced for attempting more appropriate forms. Thus, the shaping is designed to encourage replacement of appropriate linguistic forms for the often inappropriate communication (e.g. tantrums, self injury), rather than focusing on accurate direct imitation of the targets. Koegel and his colleagues have reported that this approach of reinforcing attempts is much more effective that prompting direct imitation in children with autism (see the review in Koegel, Koegel, and Dunlap 1996).

6.2 *Example of Clinical Interaction*

In order to complete natural language paradigm, the clinician must first complete a functional analysis (Carr and Durand 1985). After 'natural reinforcers' have been identified as well as potential social contexts wherein the individual child is most likely to be communicative, these elements are included in the intervention. For this example, assume that the child is motivated by painting activities, and does not engage in aversive behaviors while painting. However, also assume the child does not communicate while painting, indeed, assume that the child is reluctant to communicate. As in the examples above, the clinician sets up paintbrushes, paints, and paper, but in this case, the paintbrushes and paper are placed in front of the child while the clinician holds the paint.

(6)   Child   (gestures to paint and grunts)
        Clinician Paint! you want paint.

The clinician then delivers the paint and attempts to paint with the child. That may be the extent of trials in the first session. Subsequent sessions would include attempts to shape the child:

(7)   Child   (gestures to paint and grunts)
        Clinician Here it is, Paintbrush! What is it? Paintbrush!
        Child   Paint.
        Clinician Yes, paintbrush, here it is. (and gives brush to child)

In natural language paradigm, prompts and models are delivered (after verbal responses have been established). The interaction always includes delivery of the desired object and prompting should not be so direct as to result in tantrum or aversive behavior by the child.

6.3   Pragmatic Aspects of the Intervention

One could argue that pragmatic skills are the underlying construct of this intervention; the goal of natural language paradigm is to unravel the nuances of the social skills of the individual with autism and through intervention modify these social skills so that they more closely match appropriate forms of interaction. Functional pragmatic analysis is the initial step in the intervention and is an ongoing integral part of the intervention plan. From a broader perspective, natural language paradigm represents a shift in focus from form to function which was brought about in large measure by Koegel's observation that teaching language form alone was not altering the interaction style of most children with autism. Rather, these children would use the learned forms (often reluctantly) under tightly controlled conditions, but were not sufficiently motivated to communicate when outside the training setting. Koegel then examined the social interaction of children with autism in order to determine how they could become motivated to use the forms appropriately. Thus, the 'pragmatics' of this intervention consists of meta-analysis and overtly training the child with autism to use the targets in appropriate contexts, and more importantly, to discontinue use of inappropriate behaviors to communicate.

6.4   Relationship to Pragmatics of Generalization

Because the goal of the natural language paradigm is to directly teach appropriate social skills in children with autism, much of the training is completed in the generalization setting. Although one could argue that the training includes didactic elements that rarely occur in the generalization setting, these elements are used to directly train the language skills in the generalized home context. Thus, there is a direct relationship between the intervention and the pragmatic aspects of generalization as these are the focus of the intervention.

7.   Conversational Recast

7.1   Description of the Intervention

Conversational recast intervention is based upon the rare event learning model proposed by Nelson (1989). In this approach, the child is provided with indirect corrective feedback that is delivered immediately following their own productions (see the analysis in Moerk 1992). For example, assume the target is the auxiliary grammatical morpheme ("she is walking"). This treatment focuses on expanding the child's production to include the auxiliary (which the child is deleting in spontaneous speech). For example, if the child says "girl walk," the clinician would respond "yes, the girl is walking." No imitative prompts are delivered, rather the goal of treatment is to provide multiple examples of the target so that the child hears the expanded version immediately following his/her own attempts (Camarata *et al.* 1994; Nelson *et al.* 1996). The context for the intervention includes play materials that are selected by the child. The clinician will make available to the child (for selection) toys that are likely to elicit attempts of the targets during play interactions. Note that this approach is designed to be used with children who are already attempting to communicate using immature forms (i.e. who display at least rudimentary motivation for communication as the recasts are responses to child initiations).

7.2 *Example of Clinical Interaction:*

Once again, assume the treatment session is designed around painting activities and assume the targets are colors and two word combinations.

(8)   Clinician Let's paint a picture.
        Child   (gestures to paints)
        Clinician What?
        Child   Paint.
        Clinician Oh, you want the paint! Blue paint.
        Child   Paint, want paint.
        Clinician Yes, you want the paint. (gives paint to child) Here's the
                  blue paint.

The clinician continues to play with the child and delivers recasts whenever the child initiates:

        Child   Paint!
        Clinician More paint! Red paint! Here. (gives more paint to the
                  child)
        Child   I paint.
        Clinician Yes, with red paint.

7.3   Pragmatic Aspects of the Intervention

Conversational recast intervention differs from the approaches described above in at least one key aspect of the functional pragmatic characteristics of the procedures: recasts are exclusively delivered in response to child initiations. Because of this, the child has a more active role in the interaction as the clinician is following the child's conversational lead. In addition, this approach includes no direct prompting or requests for imitation. To be sure, play materials and clinician interactions are designed to indirectly elicit target attempts from the child, but these are quite different from a functional pragmatic perspective than the requests for imitation implemented within analog/didactic intervention, incidental teaching, and milieu teaching. Indeed, conversational recast teaching also does not include the types of prompting for social interaction included in natural language paradigm because the children examined within conversational recast do not require additional scaffolding for attempts at social interaction (as required in children with autism). Thus, the pragmatic characteristics of conversational recast include child initiations in play contexts followed by adult responses to these initiations. Because any initiation can be recast, a wide variety of pragmatic functions are observed in treatment sessions (e.g. statements, requests, descriptions, questions etc.).

7.4   Relationship to Pragmatics of Generalization

Conversational recast intervention is similar to the generalization context in a number of key aspects. First, the child is exposed to the targets in a variety of pragmatic contexts (as is the case in home settings). Indeed, the intervention is embedded in play episodes that are designed to closely parallel the description of natural language learning in parent child interactions (see Brown and Hanlon 1970, and Moerk 1992). Second, the child initiations are the trigger for delivery of recasts, such that the motivation, and attention of the child are an inherent part of the teaching episode (i.e. the child is engaged in play and is interacting positively with the clinician; see Haley, Camarata and Nelson 1994). Thus, it is not surprising that targets learned under conversational recast intervention generalize quickly across settings and across conversational partners (cf. Camarata et al. 1994) because the child is learning in contexts that are highly similar to the generalization learning situation.

8.   Whole Language

8.1   *Description of the Intervention*

Whole language intervention has arisen from an orientation to reading instruction (Norris 1990; Chaney 1990) and focuses on directly paralleling natural language acquisition. The goal of whole language instruction is to provide a supportive environment for communication, and language enrichment activities built upon 'themes' that are similar to everyday interactions in preschool settings (Hoffman, Norris, and Monjure 1990). These themes are often topic oriented, such as weather conditions, daily activities, and children's stories, rather than being goal oriented (as in the previous intervention types). Thus, whole language intervention closely resembles preschool activities for children without language disabilities and typically does not include a specific focus on language structure. There appears to be an implicit assumption that children with language learning disabilities do not require direct or indirect instruction on language structures, rather, additional nonspecific exposure to language will remediate the disability (Norris and Hoffman 1993).

8.2   *Example of Clinical Interaction*

Once again, assume the treatment session is designed around painting activities, but whole language typically includes global goals, such as increasing MLU (Norris and Hoffman 1993). A whole language session will include recasts (as these are a part of natural language interaction, Conti-Ramsden 1990), but will not include a focus on modelling, or recasting a particular set of language structures.

> (9)   Clinician Let's paint a picture. Today we are painting a horse.
> Child   (gestures to paints)
> Clinician Those are paints and we are painting the horse.
> Child   Paint.
> Clinician Blue paint. No, we should paint the horse brown. Here's the brown paint.
> Child   Paint, want paint.
> Clinician OK, here's the brown paint, let's paint the horse.

The clinician continues to play with the child and talk about the activity.
   Child Horse.

> Clinician Yes, a horse.
> Child   Brown horse.

Clinician Now lets make a black one! Here's the black paint.
Child   More paint?
Clinician Yes, let's paint this one black.

The activity continues around the theme of painting horses.

8.3 Pragmatic Aspects of the Intervention

As in conversation recast, the focus of whole language is on social communication and includes pragmatically appropriate responses to the child. The actual instructional theme is selected by the clinician who guides the child through each of the planned activities (as in preschool settings), but a key element of the intervention is to be responsive to the child (Norris and Hoffman 1993). Thus, a pragmatic analysis of whole language intervention would yield a wide variety of communicative functions from the clinician and from the child, including topic initiation and maintenance, topic shifts, comments, responses, questions and answers, and recasts of the child's productions. Whole language approaches typically do not include prompts or direct requests for imitation (Hoffman *et al.* 1990; Norris 1990). Indeed, the goal of whole language is to provide a pragmatically rich communicative environment for the child (Norris and Hoffman 1993).

8.4 Relationship to Pragmatics of Generalization

The social context of whole language directly parallels the pragmatics of the generalization setting, being particularly close to the interactions often observed in preschool settings that focus on enrichment rather than on specific instructional materials. Because the interactions are embedded in conversational contexts, there is a close match between the pragmatics of the intervention and the generalization settings. Given this close match, one may wonder why this would not be the intervention of choice when remediating child language disability. Clearly, any skills acquired within intervention are highly likely to also be used outside the intervention setting. Indeed, one could argue that there is little difference between the intervention setting and the generalization setting, and therein lies a primary criticism of whole language approaches (Camarata 1996; Chaney 1990): If a child is having difficulty acquiring language without intervention, it is perhaps unlikely that simply duplicating what is occurring in the natural language environment will be sufficient to trigger language growth. An underlying assumption in the intervention methods presented previously is that the child with language disabilities requires specialized intervention support to learn new language structures. As shown, the procedures differ with regard to the ways that the language goals are highlighted during intervention, but all provide planned support for specific language structures. In addition, because whole language methods lack specificity regarding language targets and deliver a wide variety of responses to the child, it is often difficult to determine which responses (if any) are associated with language growth. Thus, whole language intervention directly parallels the pragmatic parameters of the generalization setting, but may lack the focus on specific language structures that many children with language learning disabilities evidently require for learning. Consider the example above: the clinician provided potential teaching responses (e.g. recasting a definite article: "a horse"), but there are constant shifts in the forms recast, from grammatical morphemes (a horse) to semantic relations (blue paint) to complex sentences (those are paints and we are painting the horse). Perhaps this kind of constantly shifting response is difficult for the child to process (Nelson 1989).

9.   Conclusions

The above review indicates the wide diversity in the functional pragmatic characteristics of language intervention approaches for treating paediatric language disorders. On the one hand there are interventions designed to elicit multiple productions in very limited pragmatic contexts (analog/didactic). At the opposing end of the spectrum are interventions designed to directly parallel a broader variety of contexts (whole language, which includes no direct focus on language structure; conversational recast, which includes interaction designed to provide teaching responses within conversational contexts; and in terms of instilling social skills in children with autism, natural language paradigm). The middle ground is occupied by treatments that include prompts to highlight the language goals while also programming some flexibility in terms of context (incidental learning and milieu teaching). At this point in the development of these interventions, it is perhaps fair to say that all have demonstrated some levels of success in improving language skills and all have revealed weaknesses. A working hypothesis that emerges (see Camarata 1996) from an analysis of the interventions is that generalization will be more efficient for those approaches that are closer matches to the broader generalization context. This was seen in Koegel, Camarata, Koegel, Smith and Ben Tal (1998) who reported that targets acquired under analog/didactic intervention often failed to generalize (although there was generalization for some targets) whereas almost all targets acquired under conversational recast intervention generalized rapidly. This replicated a similar report by Camarata *et al.* (1994) for grammatical targets.

Camarata (1996) has suggested that treatment be initiated using procedures that share as many pragmatic features as possible to the generalization context and add decontextualized (more restricted pragmatic contexts) and prompting support if the child demonstrates a lack of learning under the more pragmatically diverse treatment. Thus, a child may require natural language paradigm to acquire motivation for communication and basic social skills. Another child may only require conversational recast intervention to learn whereas a child failing under this approach may require the prompting support provided by milieu teaching, incidental teaching, or analog/didactic intervention respectively. Although current literature suggests that all approaches can be successful (and/or unsuccessful), incorporating pragmatic analysis of the intervention procedures may provide important insights on the most efficient methods required to establish target use (and language growth) in generalized spontaneous language. More importantly, future studies that systematically examine the pragmatic continuum may provide a unified therapy model that allows for the most powerful intervention to be applied to each individual with speech and language disabilities.

Acknowledgements

The preparation of this chapters was supported in part by an endowment to the author from the Scottish Rite Foundation of Nashville and by grants from the US Department of Education (H023A30052 and H029C30070) and the National Institute on Deafness and Other Communication Disorders (R01NS01420; R01NS26437; P50DC03282).

References

Aram, D. 1988. "Language sequelae of unilateral brain lesions in children". In *Language, Communication and the Brain*, F. Blum (ed.), 171–197. New York: Raven Press.

Bambara, L. and Warren, S. 1993. "Massed trials revised: Appropriate applications in functional skill training". In *Strategies for Teaching Students with Mild to Severe Mental Retardation* (Vol. 5), R. Grable and S. Warren (eds), 165–190. London: Kingston Publishers.

Bates, E. 1976. *Language in Context*. New York, NY: Academic Press.

Bates, E. and MacWhinney, B. 1989. "Functionalism and the competition model". In *The Crosslinguistic Study of Sentence Processing*, B. MacWhinney and E. Bates (eds), 108–147. New York: Cambridge University Press.

Benton, A. 1964. "Developmental aphasia and brain damage". *Cortex* 1: 40–50.

Bloom, L. 1993. *The Transition from Infancy to Language: Acquiring the Power of Expression*. Cambridge: Cambridge University Press.

Bloom, L. and Lahey, M. 1978. *Language Development and Language Disorders*. New York: John Wiley and Sons.

Bohannon, N. and Warren-Leubecker, A. 1989. "Theoretical approaches to language acquisition". In *The Development of Language*, J. Berko-Gleason (ed.), 167–224. Columbus, OH: Merrill.

Brown, R. and Hanlon, C. 1970. "Derivational complexity and the order of acquisition in child's speech". In *Cognition and the Development of Language*, J. Hayes (ed). New York: John Wiley.

Camarata, S. 1991. "Assessment of oral language". In *Assessment in Special and Remedial Education*, J. Salvia and J. Ysseldyke (eds). Boston, MA: Houghton-Mifflin.

Camarata, S. 1993. "The application of naturalistic conversation training to speech production in children with speech disabilities". *Journal of Applied Behavior Analysis* 26: 173–182.

Camarata, S. 1995. "A rationale for naturalistic speech intelligibility intervention". In *Language Intervention: Preschool through the Early School Years*, M. Fey, J. Windsor, and S. Warren (eds), 63–84. Baltimore: Brookes.

Camarata, S. 1996. "On the importance of integrating naturalistic language, social intervention, and speech-intelligibility training". In *Positive Behavioral Support*, L. Koegel, R. Koegel, and G. Dunlap (eds), 333–352. Baltimore, MD: Paul Brookes Publishing Company.

Camarata, S. and Nelson, K. E. 1992. "Treatment efficiency as a function of target selection in the remediation of child language". *Clinical Linguistics and Phonetics* 6: 167–178.

Camarata, S., Nelson, K. E. and Camarata, M. 1994. "A comparison of conversation based to imitation based procedures for training grammatical structures in specifically language impaired children". *Journal of Speech and Hearing Research* 37: 1414–1423.

Carr, E. and Durand, M. 1985 "Reducing behavior problems through functional communication training". *Journal of Applied Behavior Analysis* 18: 111–126.

Chaney, C. 1990. "Evaluating the whole language approach to language arts: Pros and cons". *Language, Speech, and Hearing Services in Schools* 21: 244–249.

Chomsky, N. 1982. *Some Concepts and Consequences of the Theory of Government and Binding*. Cambridge, Mass.: MIT Press.

Connell, P. 1987. "Teaching language rules as solutions to language problems: A baseball analogy". *Language, Speech, and Hearing Services in Schools* 18: 194–205.

Connell, P., and Stone, C. 1992. "Morpheme learning of children with specific language impairment under controlled instructional conditions". *Journal of Speech and Hearing Research* 35: 844–852.

Conti-Ramsden, G. 1990. "Maternal recasts and other contingent replies to language-impaired children". *Journal of Speech and Hearing Disorders* 55: 262–274.

Crystal, D. 1987. "Towards a bucket theory of language disability: taking account of interaction between linguistic levels". *Clinical Linguistics and Phonetics* 1: 7–21.

Curtiss, S. 1977. *Genie: A Psycholinguistic Study of a Modern Day "Wild Child."* London: Academic Press.

Dore, J. 1974. "A pragmatic description of early language development." *Journal of Psycholinguistic Research* 4: 343–350.

Fey, M. 1986. *Language Intervention With Young Children*. San Diego: College-Hill.

Fey, M., Cleave, P. and Long, S. 1997. "Two models of grammar facilitation in children with language impairments". *Journal of Speech, Language, and Hearing Research* 40: 5–19.

Fey, M., Windsor, J. and Warren, S. 1995. *Language Intervention: Preschool through the Early School Years*. Baltimore: Brookes Publishing Company.

Gray, B. and Ryan, B. 1973. *A Language Program for the Nonlanguage Child*. Champaign, IL: Research Press.

Haley, K., Camarata, S. and Nelson, K. 1994. "Social valence in specifically language impaired children during imitation based and conversation based language intervention". *Journal of Speech and Hearing Research* 37: 378–388.

Hart, B., Reynolds, N., Baer, D., Brawley, E. and Harris, F. 1968. "Effect of contingent and noncontingent social reinforcement on the cooperative play of a preschool child". *Journal of Applied Behavior Analysis* 1: 73–76.

Hart, B. and Risley, T. 1968. "Establishing use of descriptive adjectives in the spontaneous speech of disadvantaged preschool children". *Journal of Applied Behavior Analysis* 1: 109–120.

Hart, B. and Risley, T. 1995. *Meaningful Differences in the Everyday Experiences of Young American Children*. Baltimore: Brookes.

Hart, B. and Rogers-Warren, A. 1978. "A milieu approach to teaching language. In *Language Intervention Strategies*, R. Schiefelbusch (ed.). Baltimore: University Park Press.

Hoffman, P., Norris, J. and Monjure, J. 1990. "Comparison of process targeting and whole language treatments for phonologically delayed preschool children". *Language, Speech, and Hearing Services in Schools* 21: 102–109.

Kaiser, A. 1993. "Enhancing children's social communication". In *Enhancing Children's Communication: Research Foundations for Intervention*, A. Kaiser and D. Grey (eds), 3–9. Baltimore: Brookes.

Kaiser, A. and Hester, P. 1994. "Generalized effects of enhanced milieu teaching". *Journal of Speech and Hearing Research* 37: 1320–1340.

Kirk, S. and Chalfant, S. 1984. *Academic Development and Learning Disabilities*. Denver, CO: Lowe Publishing Company.

Kirk, S. and Kirk, W. 1971. *Psycholinguistic Learning Disabilities*. Urbana, IL: University of Illinois Press.

Koegel, R., Camarata, S., Koegel, L., Smith, A. and Ben Tal, A. (1998). "Naturalistic speech-intelligibilty teaching". *Journal of Autism and Developmental Disabilities* 28: 241–251.

Koegel, R., O'Dell, M. and Koegel, L. 1987. "A natural language teaching paradigm for nonverbal autistic children". *Journal of Autism and Developmental Disorders* 17: 187–200.

Koegel, L., Koegel, R. and Dunlap, G. 1996. *Positive Behvavioral Support*. Baltimore: Brookes Publishing Company.

Lahey, M. 1988. *Language Development and Language Disorders*. New York: MacMillan.

Leonard, L., Camarata, S., Schwartz, R., Rowan, L. and Chapman, K. 1982. "The communicative functions of lexical usage by language impaired children". *Applied Psycholinguistics* 3: 109–125.

McReynolds, L. 1987. "A perspective on articulation generalization". *Seminars in Speech and Language* 8: 217–240.

Miller, J. 1981. *Assessing Language Production in Children*. Austin: Pro-Ed.

Moerk, E. 1992. *A first Language Taught and Learned*. Baltimore, MD: Brookes Publishing Company.

Mowrer, D. 1984. "Behavioural approaches to treating language disorders". In *Remediating Children's Language: Behavioural and Naturalistic Approaches*, D. Müller (ed.), 18–54. San Diego, CA: College-Hill.

Muma, J. 1978. *Language Handbook: Concepts, Assessment and Intervention*. Englewood Cliffs, NJ: Prentice-Hall.

Myklebust, H. 1971. "Childhood aphasia: An evolving concept". In *Handbook of Speech Pathology and Audiology*, L. Travis (ed), 1181–1202. Englewood Cliffs, NJ: Prentice-Hall.

Nelson, K. E. 1989. "Strategies for first language teaching". In *The Teachability of Language*, M. Rice and R. Schiefelbusch (eds), Baltimore: Brookes.

Nelson, K. E., Camarata, S. M., Welsh, J., Butkovsky, L., and Camarata, M. 1996. "Effects of imitative and conversational recasting treatment on the acquisition of grammar in children with Specific Language Impairment and younger language-normal children. *Journal of Speech and Hearing Research* 39: 850–859.

Norris, J. 1990. "Whole language in theory and practice: Implications for language intervention". *Language, Speech, and Hearing Services in Schools* 21: 212- 220.

Norris, H. and Hoffman, P. 1993. *Whole Language Intervention for School Age Children*. San Diego, CA: Singular Publishing.

Owens, R. 1991. *Language Disorders: A Functional Approach to Assessment and Intervention*. New York: Merril.

Pinker, S. 1995. *The Language Instinct*. New York: Harper Collins.

Plante, E., Swisher, L., Vance, R. and Rapcak, S. 1991. "MRI findings in boys with specific language impairment". *Brain and Language* 41: 67–80.

Prizant, B. M., Audet, L. R., Burke, G., Hummel, L., Maher, S. and Theadore, G. 1993. "Communication disorders and emotional/behavioral disorders in children and adolescents". *Journal of Speech and Hearing Disorders* 58.

Prutting, C. 1979. "Process: The action of moving forward progressively from one point to another on the way to completion". *Journal of Speech and Hearing Disorders* 44: 3–30.

Prutting, C. and Kirchner, D. 1987. "A clinical appraisal of the pragmatic aspects of language". *Journal of Speech and Hearing Disorders* 52: 105–19.

Searle, J. 1969. *Speech Acts*. Cambridge: Cambridge University Press.

Skinner, B. 1957. *Verbal Behavior*. New York: Apple, Century, Crofts.

Tomblin, B. 1989. "Familial concentration of developmental language impairment". *Journal of Speech and Hearing Disorders* 54: 587–595.

Warren, S. and Kaiser, A. 1986. "Incidental language teaching: A critical review". *Journal of Speech and Hearing Disorders* 51: 291–299.

Warren, S., McQuarters, R. and Rogers-Warren, A. 1984. "The effects of mands and models on the speech of unresponsive language delayed preschool children". *Journal of Speech and Hearing Disorders* 49: 43–52.

Wyatt, G. 1969. *Language Learning and Communication Disorders in Children*. New York, Free Press.

Name Index

Subject Index

In the STUDIES IN SPEECH PATHOLOGY AND CLINICAL LINGUISTICS (SSPCL) series the following titles have been published thus far:

1. KENT, Raymond D. (ed.): *Intelligibility in Speech Disorders. Theory, measurement and management.* 1992.
2. CLAHSEN, Harald: *Child Language and Developmental Dysphasia. Linguistic studies of the acquisition of German. Translated from the German by Karin Richman.* 1991.
3. WRAY, Alison: *The Focusing Hypothesis. The theory of left hemisphere lateralised language re-examined.* 1992
4. WILCOX, Sherman: *The Phonetics of Fingerspelling.* 1992.
5. MENN, Lise, M. O'CONNOR, Loraine K. OBLER and Audrey HOLLAND: *Non-fluent Aphasia in a Multilingual World.* 1995.
6. BALL, Martin J. and Martin DUCKWORTH (eds): *Advances in Clinical Phonetics.* 1996.
7. MÜLLER, Nicole (ed.): *Pragmatics in Speech and Language Pathology. Studies in clinical applications.* 2000.